The Barcza-Larsen Defense

Paul H. Fields

National Master

1991

Coraopolis, Pennsylvania

Chess Enterprises

ISBN: 0-945470-17-7

Editor: B. G. Dudley

Cover Design: E. F. Witalis, Jr.

Typesetting by the author

Proofreading: Thomas Magar

Contents

Preface

This games collection is designed for the player of the Black pieces who enjoys exploring less-traveled roads in the openings. Although many famous grandmasters will be found defending the Barcza-Larsen in the pages that follow, this defense has never been studied with the microscopic attention accorded many other opening variations. There are no comprehensive works or specialized monographs available; this collection represents an attempt to bring together, for the first time, a substantial number of games demonstrating the various strategies relevant to this system. It is the author's hope that study of this material will provide both aesthetic enjoyment as well as tournament points.

No one can claim only personal credit for producing a new book, and that is certainly the case with the present volume. Besides mentioning the many wonderful players whose efforts form the basis for this work, I would particularly like to thank Dr. Alice N. Loranth and Dr. Motoko B. Reece of the Cleveland Public Library, Special Collections, John G. White Chess Collection. Without their kind assistance, and that of their staff, this book would not have been written. And, as Dr. Reece thoughtfully pointed out, without the generosity of Mr. John G. White, a great patron of chess, much of this material would have remained inaccessible. My thanks to them, and, finally, to my dear wife Karen, whose encouragement helped make this possible.

Paul H. Fields
Tampa, Florida
February 1991

References

Alt-Benoni Verteidigung, by Stoljar & Kondratiev
Batsford Chess Openings, 1st & 2nd Ed.
Benoni, by Hartston
Ben-Oni Defence, by Gelenczei
The British Chess Magazine, 1957-89
Ceskoslovensky Sach, Vol. 50-83
Chess Digest, Vol. 3, by Morgan
Chess/Pergamon Chess, Vol. 21-55
Chess Life/Chess Life & Review, Vol. 1-46
Chess Olympiad Skopje '72, by Matanovic
Chess Openings: Theory & Practice, by Horowitz
Deutsche Schachzeitung, 1957-89
Encyclopedia of Chess Openings, Vol. A
Fernschach, Vol. 1-50
47th USSR Championships 1979, by Miles
Helsinki Olmpiad 1952, (Bulletins)
Jaenisch's Chess Openings, by Jaenisch
Magyar Sakkelet, Vol. 1-37
Modern Chess Openings, 12th & 13th Ed.
Neue Eroffnungswege, by Gunderam
New in Chess, Vol. 1-18 & Keybook
Oxford Companion to Chess, by Hooper & Whyld
Oxford Encyclopedia of Chess Games, Vol. 1,
        by Levy & O'Connell
Revistah de Sah, Vol. 7-40
Sahovski Informator, Vol. 1-50
San Antonio 1972, by Larsen & Levy
Schach, Vol. 10-43
Shakhmaty v. USSR, Vol. 34-66
Siegen Olympiad 1970, (Bulletins)
Skak, 1954-71
Skakbladet, Vol. 1-84
Tournament Chess, Vol. 1-35
Unorthodox Openings, by Benjamin & Schiller

Symbols

Algebraic notation has been used throughout the text. As a shorthand aid to the reader, game headings automatically indicate the result, for example, Game 1: Minchin+Trelawny indicates White won; Game 36 Filip-Barcza indicates Black won; and Game 72: Jonsson=Horvath indicates a draw. Game fragments incorporated within the notes, such as 'Campora/Cebalo, Vrsac 1981' merely indicate the players, event, and date, without indicating the result.

Other symbols used:

+	Check
++	Double check
+=	White is slightly better
=+	Black is slightly better
+-	White has a distinct advantage
-+	Black has a distinct advantage
>	With the idea of...

What's in a Name?

This is a book about an opening with a tortured nomenclature. It has been referred to as the Franco-Sicilian, Franco-Benoni, Benoni, Irregular French, just plain Irregular, and our name of choice, the Barcza-Larsen Defense. Some sources offer no name at all.

In choosing to follow the custom of naming an opening after top-level practitioners, I think the following games and analysis will confirm these two world-class players had a special understanding of the nuances of this system. But before we delve into the mysteries of the Barcza-Larsen, let's meet the masters after whom the defense is named.

Bent Larsen (1935-   ) may need no introduction. The Danish International Grandmaster (1956) is a four-time World Championship Candidates qualifier and one of the finest tournament players in the history of the game. Well-known for his aggressive, optimistic approach, Larsen has always played to win. During his lengthy career, he has consistently employed old and forgotten openings, often adding his personal touch to bring out unexpected venom in a variation long thought innocuous. He has written, in this regard, "I do not deliberately play openings that are obviously bad. I emphasize the surprise element, and in some cases this makes me play a variation without being absolutely convinced that it is correct."

Happily, the Great Dane was in good company when he trusted in the correctness of the Barcza-Larsen Defense. Greats like Staunton, Anderssen, Spielmann, Uhlmann, Hubner, Evans, Kavalek, and even Gary Kasparov have played the defense, as did the man responsible for its modern introduction, Gedeon Barcza.

Gedeon Barcza (1911-1986), pronounced BART-sa), was a Hungarian International Grandmaster (1954) and International Correspondence Chess Master (1966). He won the Hungarian national championship eight times, represented his country in seven Olympiads, and participated in two Interzonal tournaments (1952 and 1962). He had a fine, positionally-based feel for closed openings, and the debut for White that bears his name, the Barcza System (1.Nf3 2.g3 3.Bg2 4.O-O, intending a later c4), sometimes thought of as part of the Reti Opening, clearly exemplified his style of play. His positional interpretation of the Barcza-Larsen Defense was very different from Bent Larsen's counter-attacking approach, yet both players enjoyed successes with their respective methods.

This diversity within the Barcza-Larsen Defense may help explain why it has been employed by strategists and tacticians alike, and why theorists of the unexplored like Basman, Diemer and Gunderam have taken a special interest in its complications. And now, you too will help forge the theory of this interesting line. Many happy games!

A Theoretical Introduction

Why play the Barcza-Larsen Defense? The best reason may be to take advantage of an opening system that can be employed (on occasion) against both 1.e4 and 1.d4, thereby minimizing the amount of opening study required to prepare as Black. It's important to ensure that the opening you study really stands a good chance of being used in actual play; if the path to your system is not 'narrow', your opponent may bypass your opening preparation in the first few moves.

Let's take a look at the introductory moves of the Barcza-Larsen Defense.

1.e4   e6   Against 1.e4, this is the best way to get to the Barcza-Larsen, since White replies with 2.d4 most of the time, anticipating a 'normal' French Defense. Against 1.d4, Black may try 1...c5 2.d5 e6. (old Benoni A43)

2.d4   c5   With this move, Black renounces any intentions of entering the French Defense. The theoretically approved move for White is now 3.d5, grabbing space and trying to cramp the Black position. White's main option is 3.Nf3, trying to transpose into an open Sicilian where Black must play a system based on ...e6. The good news for Black is, despite being out of the Barcza-Larsen, he has avoided the many White anti-Sicilian systems such as the Closed (2.Nc3), Grand Prix (2.f4), Sveshnikov/Alapin (2.c3), Smith-Morra (2.d4), etc. Advice for Black? Pick an ...e6-Sicilian system that mirrors the way you play the Barcza-Larsen or experiment with 3...a6 (hoping to entice 4.d5), 3...d5 (the Marshall variation of the Sicilian), or even 3...b6. As we will see, the Barcza-Larsen can be played as a clear, positionally-based line or as a complicated counter-attacking system.

3.d5   As previously mentioned, White plays this move to control more space by advancing across the middle of the board, thereby inhibiting the development of Black's pieces, notably the Nc8 (which is denied the use of the c6 square). The Black Bf8 is also somewhat restricted by the Black pawn on c5. Black's piece set-up, however, can be flexibly altered to make a target of the advanced White pawn on d5.

3...   exd5   Black can delay (or omit) this move by, for example, playing ...Nf6 (or ...d6) first, but the pawn exchange ...exd5 is central to the defensive concept of the Barcza-Larsen, and from a practical standpoint, White scores well when Black refrains from ...exd5. Nevertheless, adventurous spirits may find much of interest in 3...g6, the Gunderam variation, where Black quickly fianchettoes king-side and dares White to occupy the center. This system has much in common with Lothar Schmid's interpretation of the Benoni Defense; indeed, direct transposition is often possible. While the bulk of grandmaster practice has not featured ...g6, the early fianchetto may prove a viable alternative to other traditional developmental schemes. Going back to our examination of the main line Barcza-Larsen: after 3...exd5, 4.exd5 is virtually forced, else White loses time with his queen after an eventual ...Nf6.

4.exd5   d6   Black 'fixes' the central pawn structure and provides for the development of the Bc8. White is given the opportunity to support the d5 pawn not by playing c4, but by playing Nc3 instead, thereby leaving the c4 square vacant for use by another piece, usually the king's knight, which makes use of the maneuver Ng1-f3-d2-c4. This developmental idea, which is so important to QP Benoni systems, is equally relevant to the Barcza-Larsen, but an important difference between the openings should be noted. In a traditional QP Benoni, White has recaptured on d5 with the c-pawn, thereby creating rival pawn majorities (for White, on the king-side; for Black, on the queen-side). In the Barcza-Larsen, however, there are no rival pawn majorities; the opposing pawn structures are evenly distributed. Furthermore, the e-file is open, permitting exchange of heavy pieces- the rooks and queens. Black, therefore, will not have to worry about his king being overrun by a White pawn storm on the king-side, as often happens in a QP Benoni. On the other hand, Black's counterplay is not as sharply based. He must find alternative means to attack the White position.

5.Nc3   This is White's most flexible move. While it does preclude the pawn advance c4, that move would take the c4 square from White's pieces and restrict the Bf1. There is an additional reason for 5.Nc3, instead of, say, 5.Nf3 - White wishes to deny Black the exchanging maneuver ...Bc8-g4x(Nf3), which was often employed by the originator of the defense, Gedeon Barcza. For example, by playing Bf1-e2 before Ng1-f3, White can counter ...Bc8-g4 by simply playing Nf3-d2, offering to exchange light-squared bishops (normally in White's favor) and heading for c4 with the knight. Barcza's relinquishing of the 'minor exchange' (Black Bc8 for White Ng1) would appear to be justified by the fixed White pawn at d5, which limits the scope of White's light-squared bishop. The classic implementation of this idea came in the stem-game Filip-Barcza, Sofia 1957, (see Game 36) wherein Barcza won a good knight vs. bad bishop ending.

Does this mean that White invariably avoids 5.Nf3? No! Many players of the White pieces have employed 5.Nf3, apparently satisfied with the prospect of obtaining the 'advantage' of the two bishops. And White may not relish the thought of Black playing ...b6 and ...Bb7, attacking the advanced d5 pawn.

5   ...Nf6   Well, you might be wondering where Black is going to develop the Bf8. Why not play 5...g6 instead, followed by fianchettoing with ...Bg7? The answer lies in the form of Black's backward pawn on d6. With a Black bishop on g7, the d6 pawn might become a liability, should White play Bf4 and Nc4. Even so, some radical theorists (such as Gunderam) have advocated the ...g6 fianchetto here, too, after 'adequate' preparation, which usually involves ...a7-a6 and the fanciful maneuvers ...f7-f6, ...Nb8-d7-e5, and ...Ng8-h6-f7. This 'strong-point' approach, based on establishing a knight at e5 (thereby shielding the weak d6 pawn), has been employed against White set-ups with a pawn at c4 (as in the traditional Benoni) or a knight at c4 (as in the Barcza-Larsen or 1.d4 c5 Benoni, where White refrains from c2-c4.) When Black does not fianchetto, preferring to develop with 5...Ng8-f6 and 6...Bf8-e7, he directly supports the d6 pawn and prepares to castle. After castling, Black's king's rook will come to e8, contesting the open file by permitting the retreat ...Be7-f8. The ultimate positioning of Black's king's bishop on its original square may appear odd at first sight, but from f8 it serves the dual function of supporting the d6 pawn and defending Black's king. And the subsequent maneuver ...g6 and ...Bg7 is still available, should the opportunity arise. This kind of 'delayed fianchettoing' is reminiscent of certain variations in the Spanish Game (the Ruy Lopez).

6.Be2   The most 'exact', denying the ...Bc8-g4x(Nf3) exchanging maneuver. Alternatively, White has sometimes played 6.Bb5+, hoping to provoke ...Bd7. White would then exchange light-squared bishops (since Black's bishop is a little better), eliminating any possibility of a later bad bishop vs. good knight ending. Black, however, is not compelled to answer Bb5+ with ...Bd7, and, instead, can play ...Nbd7, blocking the check and preparing to kick the Bb5 with ...a6. Should White then opt for the exchange Bb5xNd7, Black would be left with the two bishops. And if White answers ...a6 by retreating the Bb5, Black can expand with ...b5.

6.   **...Be7**
7.Nf3   **O-O**

8.O-O   Some sources, such as Estrin, consider this to be a mistake, marking it with ?!. Evidently, the theorists wish to prevent any active development of the Bc8 (by playing 8.Nd2) but, as we have seen, Black has no desire to exchange light-squared bishops (which would occur after 8.O-O Bg4 9.Nd2 anyway).

8.   **... Na6**   When you see this move for the first time, it looks bad. Can't White just play Be2xNa6, destroying Black's queen-side pawn structure? Sure, but for the resulting doubled and isolated a-pawns, Black gets something in return - the half-open b-file for his rook, the two bishops, and the possibility of controlling the a6-f1 diagonal by playing ...a5 and ...Ba6. By playing 8...Na6, Black prepares to play the knight to c7, pressuring the d5 pawn, leaving the c8-h3 diagonal unblocked (instead of clogging it with the passive 8...Nbd7) and envisions further pressure on the d5 pawn by ...b6 and ...Bb7. A knight on c7 may also offer support for the subsequent tactical thrust ...b5. This is the more complicated, counter-attacking interpretation of the Barcza-Larsen favored by grandmasters such as Larsen himself. As Gligoric has noted, Black's basic strategy is to surround and continually harass the advanced d5 pawn, maintaining tension in the position.

At this point, White has some options. He may play 9.Bf4, attacking the backward pawn at d6; 9.Re1, preparing to contest the e-file; 9.h3, limiting the scope of the Black Bc8; or 9.a3, which, coupled with Rb1 and/or b4, envisions queen-side expansion and domination of the b-file. White has even tried 9.Nb5, attempting to prevent Black's regrouping maneuver ...Na6-c7, although this idea appears a bit artificial. Regardless, Black obtains a playable game. By remembering Steinitz's dictum that cramped positions must be freed slowly, Black can gradually but inexorably expand with moves like ...Nc7, ...b6, ...Re8, ...Bf8, and ...Bb7. 'Creeping' moves like ...h6 (preventing a White bishop from settling on g5 and threatening Bg5x(N)f6, wrecking the Black king-side pawns), and ...a6, (keeping White pieces out of b5 and also preparing for queen-side expansion) come into consideration. The Black queen is often well-posted at d7, controlling light squares and eyeing the f5 square, from where it would threaten the White pawn on d5. The Black rooks are sometimes exchanged off along the open e-file for their White counterparts; Black does not object to the bloodletting as long as the pressure is maintained on d5.

It's interesting to note that in Larsen's games, the Danish grandmaster sometimes deferred playing ...Bc8-b7, hoping for a more active placement for his bishop, for example, on the f5 square. But even when ...Bc8-b7 had been played, Larsen did not feel constrained to accept a one-dimensional role for this piece.   Indeed, in Hamilton-Larsen (Game 55) Black's bishop was first played to b7, tying down White's pieces to the defence of the d5 pawn, and then redeployed by the maneuver ...Bb7-c8-f5, a good example of flexibility in thinking and the ability to keep looking for optimal piece placement.

Meanwhile, White is not sitting by idly. White players often employ the pawn advance a2-a4 to hamper any queen-side ambition by Black. The a2-a4 thrust practically compels Black to immediately play ...b6, if he has not already done so, the reason being that White would be delighted with the

12

opportunity to play a4-a5, further cramping Black and threatening (after a later ...b6 by Black) a5xb6 at a potentially awkward moment.

A different White queen-side plan is to play a3, Rb1, and b4, followed by b4xc5, trying to dominate the b-file. This plan is similar to a White strategy against the Czech Benoni (QP Benoni with ...e5).

Although White often plays Nf3-d2-c4 to further menace the d6 pawn, White can also play (after h3) Nf3-h2-g4, a prophylactic strategy designed to swap off the Black Nf6, one of the pieces attacking d5. Alternatively, White may play to post the Nf3 at f5 (via the h4 square), trying to provoke the 'weakening' pawn move ...g6.

White's rooks are often placed at d1 and e1, and are sometimes doubled on the e-file. As previously mentioned, Black can try to defuse the pressure along the e-file by exchanging off rooks.

When White has played h2-h3 to limit the scope of Black's Bc8, White can consider further gripping the light squares by playing g2-g4 and Be2-f3. This strategy was seen in Diez del Corral-Fuller, (Game 57), and is basically a containment policy (although Black does need to prepare for the potential pawn advance g4-g5 by providing a flight square for the Nf6 with ...h6).

Finally, let's look at a typical position where Black is ready, after continually harassing White, to eat the pawn on d5. This is given as an introductory warning - even when Black has apparently succeeded in carrying out the surrounding strategy, there may still be pitfalls. The following diagram shows Black about to make his 21st move in the game D. Gurevich-Kavelek (Game 73):

(See diagram at the top of the next page)

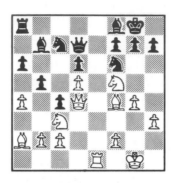

Kavalek played 21...Ncxd5, and after 22.Nxd5, recaptured with 22...Nxd5?, which seemed natural enough, but he overlooked 23.Bxd6! Black went on to draw the game after a reciprocal innacuracy by White, but Black could have safely grabbed the d5 pawn by playing 22...Bxd5! instead (23.Bg5 Bb7 24.Bxf6 Qc6 25.Kf1 Qg2+ 26.Ke2 gxf6 and Black is better).

The moral? Keep up the pressure on d5, but look twice before snatching the pawn! The difference between a safe snatch and a regrettable grab may be slight indeed.

A Note on Move Order

The Barcza-Larsen may be reached from a variety of direct and transpositional routes. As previously noted, 1.e4 e6 2.d4 c5 offers the best chance for Black to get what he wants (3.d5); however, 1.d4 c5 2.d5 e6 3.e4 amounts to the same thing, as does 1. d4 e6 2. e4 c5 3. d5.

Transpositions can arise from the Veresov Opening: 1.d4 Nf6 2.Nc3 c5 3.d5 e6 4.e4 exd5 5.exd5 d6; Queen's Pawn without c2-c4: 1.d4 Nf6 2.Nf3 c5 3.d5 d6 4.Nc3 e6 5.e4 (or 5.Bb5+/5.dxe6); the Schmid Benoni: 1.d4 c5 2.d5 d6 3.Nc3 Nf6 4.e4 e6 5.Nf3 exd5 6.exd5; and even the Sicilian Defense, Smith-Morra Gambit: 1.e4 c5 2.d4 e6 (!).

It was not difficult sorting games that arrived at the 'main line' Barcza-Larsen position after 1.e4 e6 2.d4 c5 3.d5 exd5 4.exd5 d6 5.Nf3 Nf6 6.Nc3 Be7 etc., (regardless of transpositional route); however, dealing with games featuring the Gunderam variation presents a different problem, namely, where does the Gunderam variation end and the Modern Benoni proper begin? For example, after 1.e4 e6 2.d4 c5 3.d5 g6 Black often defers exd5 until after White has played c4. Sometimes White plays exd5, reaching a 'normal' Barcza-Larsen pawn structure, but sometimes White plays cxd5, as in the Modern Benoni. To solve this problem, I have included some games where White played cxd5 but Black gave the game independent flavor by playing ...Ne7 rather than ...Nf6, avoiding transposition to the Modern Benoni.

Chapter 1: Early Deviations

1A: Black plays ...g6, delaying or omitting ...exd5: The Gunderam Variation

Game 1: Minchin+Trelawny, London 1866

1.e4 e6 2.d4 c5 3.d5 g6 If Black is determined to fianchetto, doing so before playing ...exd5 and ...d6 at least has the merit of avoiding a weak d6-pawn. Black's reasoning behind an immediate 3...g6, instead of ...d6 first, is to sidestep White's potentially awkward Bf1-b5+. But 3...g6 gives White the opportunity to muddy the waters with 4.d6!?, driving a wedge into Black's position. The question then, is, will the advanced pawn be strong or weak? One direct approach for Black would be 4...e5?! and 5...Qb6, although White may be able to defend the d6-pawn with Nb1-a3-c4. Another try is 4...f6!?, envisioning 5.f4 Nh6! 6.Nf3 (6.e5 fxe5 7.fxe5 Qh4+) 6...Nf7 7.e5 fxe5 8.fxe5 Bg7 9.Bf4 Nc6 and White has difficulty keeping his center intact; 10.Qe2 is met by 10...g5! and 11...g4!, while 10. Nc3 encourages Black to expand on the queen-side with 10...a6 and 11...b5. It is interesting to note that in the foregoing variation, Black's attack ultimately comes against the base of White's pawn chain, in accord with true Nimzowitschian principles, albeit 60 years before the publication of My System. **4.Nf3 Bg7 5.Be2 Nf6 6.Nc3 Qa5?** A pointless excursion, since White can easily defend his e4-pawn by simply castling out of the pin. **7.O-O a6** 7...O-O was definitely necessary. **8.dxe6** Lowenthal recommended 8.d6, which is a good positional idea now that the pin on the Nc3 has been broken; however, White's choice will force Black into contortions. **8...dxe6 9.Qd6 Nbd7 10.Bg5 Bf8** Squirming. **11.Qf4 Nh5 12.Qh4 h6 13.Bd2 Qc7 14.e5?!** Overly optimistic; Black can safely take the pawn, with best defense. Unfortunately, that does not occur. **14...Nxe5 15.Nxe5 Qxe5 16.Qa4+ Bd7** 16...b5?? 17.Bxb5+ **17.Bb5**

17...Rd8? 17...O-O-O! or 17...Bxb5 18.Nxb5 O-O-O! would have enabled Black to organize an adequate defense. **18.Bxd7+ Rxd7 19.Rfe1 Qd4 20.Qb3?** White overestimates his potential along the d-file and offers an unsound sacrifice... **20...c4?!** ...which Black unwisely declines! After 20...Qxd2! 21.Rad1 Qf4 22.Rxd7 Kxd7 23.Qxb7+ Qc7 24.Rd1+ Bd6! Black can maintain his piece advantage and win. **21.Qa4 Qb6** Now it's too late to take the Bd2; e.g., 21...Qxd2 22.Rad1 b5 23.Qxa6 > 24.Rxd7 & 25.Rd1 +- **22.Be3 Qc6** Black breaks the pressure but ends up with a shattered queen-side. **23.Qxc6 bxc6 24.Ne4** >25.g4 **24...f5** And now the e6 pawn is weak, too. **25.Nc3 Kf7 26.Na4 Bb4 27.c3 Be7 28.Bc5 Nf4 29.Bxe7 Rxe7 30.Rad1 Nd3 31.Re2 Rd7 32.Nb6 Rd5!?** A good practical try, but White just laughs and ignores winning the exchange; gobbling isolated pawns is an easier win. **33.Nxc4 Nf4 34.Red2 Rhd8 35.g3 Rxd2 36.Rxd2 Rxd2 37.Nxd2 Nd3 38.Nc4 Kf6** 38...e5 > ...Ke6 was better. **39.Kf1 e5 40.Ke2 Nc5 41.f3 f4 42.Nd6 fxg3 43.hxg3 Na4 44.Ne4+ Ke7 45.b3 Nb6 46.c4 Nd7 47.a4 a5 48.Kd3 Ke6 49.Kc3 c5 50.Kd3 h5 51.Ke3 Ke7 52.f4 Ke6 53.Kf3 Kf5** Black is in Zugzwang. **54.Nd6+ Ke6 55.Nb7 Kf5 56.fxe5 Nxe5+ 57.Kg2 Nd3 58.Nxa5 Nc1 59.Nc6 Nxb3 60.a5 Nd4 61.Nxd4+ cxd4 62.a6 Black Resigns.**

Game 2: Mason+Anderssen, Paris 1878

1.e4 e6 2.d4 c5 3.d5 a6 This turns out to be a waste of time, since White can now play 4.c4, reinforcing the d5 pawn and simultaneously stopping any queen-side expansion by

Black.   **4.c4 d6   5.Nc3 g6   6.Bd3 Ne7   7.Nge2 Bg7   8.O-O O-O 9.Qb3**   9.f4, with added central control, was better.   **9...Nd7 10.Bf4 e5**   Black seals up the center before starting dark-square play on the king-side.   **11.Bg3 g5!   12.Qc2 Ng6   13.f3 Nf6 14.Nd1 Nh5   15.Be1 Nhf4   16.Nxf4 exf4   17.Rb1**   White logically counters by playing on the queen-side.   **17...Ne5   18.b4 cxb4 19.Bxb4**   The customarily weak d6 pawn is attacked from a different direction.   **19...b5   20.c5 a5   21.Bc3 Nxd3   22.Bxg7 Kxg7   23.Qxd3 dxc5   24.Qxb5 Ba6   25.Qb2+ f6   26.Rf2 Qe7 27.Qa3 g4   28.Rc2 Rfc8   29.Rbc1 Rab8   30.Qxa5 Bd3   31.Rd2 c4   32.Nf2 g3   33.hxg3 fxg3   34.Ng4   34.Nxd3? cxd3   35.Rdd1 (35.Rxc8?? Rb1+)   35...Qe5!   34...Kg6   35.Ne3 Qe5   36.Nf5 Rb7   37.Rdd1 Rb2   38.Qa7!**

38...Rc7   Defending against 39.Qg7+, but...   **39.Qe3 Kf7   40.f4!** And the queen runs out of squares- if 40...Qe8, 41.Nd6+ **40...Rxg2+**   Spite.   **41.Kxg2 Qb2+   42.Kxg3** and Black Resigns.

Game 3: Rubinstein-Spielmann, Pistyan 1912

1.d4 c5   2.d5 d6   3.c4 g6   4.e4 Bg7   5.Bd3 e6   6.Nc3 Ne7 A modern approach from eighty years ago, by a past master of romantic play!   **7.Ne2**   7.f4 exd5   8.exd5 O-O   9.Nf3 Re8 10.O-O Bf5, and Black has a good position; in contrast to the Four Pawns Attack in the King's Indian Defense, Black's ...Ne7 maneuver keeps the h8-a1 diagonal open, leaves his f7-pawn unobstructed, and permits the 'opposing' development of the Bc8.   White alternatives do not promise much: 8.cxd5 O-O 9.Nf3 a6   10.a4 Bg4   11.a5 Nd7, planning an eventual ...f5; 8.Nxd5 Nxd5   9.cxd5 O-O   10.Nf3 Bg4; nor does delaying the

18

development of the Bf1, as in the analagous variations 1.e4 e6 2.d4 c5 3.d5 g6 4.c4 Bg7 5.Nc3 d6 6.f4 Ne7 7.Nf3 exd5 8.Nxd5 Nxd5 9.exd5 O-O 10.Bd3 Re8 11.O-O Bg4, followed by ...Bxf3 and ...Nd7-f6, or 8.Nxd5 Nxd5 9.Qxd5?! Qe7 10.Be3 Nc6 11.O-O-O O-O 12.Qxd6 Qxe4 13.Bxc5 (13.Qxc5 b6 14.Bd3 Qe8!) 13...Rd8 14.Qxd8+ Nxd8 15.Rxd8+ Bf8 16.Bxf8 Bf5! 7...exd5 8.exd5 Nd7 9.f4 Nf6 10.Ng3 An unhappy outpost, since Black is able to drive away the knight with an energetic pawn thrust. 10...h5 11.O-O h4 12.Nge4 Nxe4 13.Bxe4 Bd4+ 14.Kh1 Nf5 With the insidious threat 15...Ng3+! 16.hxg3 hxg3+ 15.Bxf5 Bxf5 16.Re1+ Kf8 The momentary displacement of Black's king is only a slight inconvenience. 17.Qf3 h3 Causing a fatal weakening of White's light squares. 18.g3 Qd7 19.Bd2 Bg4 20.Qf1 Qf5 21.Rac1 Kg7 22.Be3 Bf6 23.b3 Rhe8 24.Bf2 Bf3+ 25.Kg1 Bg2

26.Rxe8 Bxf1 27.Rxa8 The two rooks obtained for White's queen cannot compensate for the insecure position of the White king. 27...Qd3 28.Re8 Qf3! 29.Kxf1 Qh1+ 30.Bg1 Qg2+ 31.Ke1 Qxg1+ 32.Kd2 Qxh2+ White Resigns.

Game 4: Van Scheltinga-Schmid, Dublin Zonal 1957

1.d4 c5 2.d5 d6 Schmid has championed this Benoni move-order throughout his career. The present game is included as an example of play which could have arisen from 1.e4 e6 2.d4 c5 3.d5 g6 3.e4 g6 4.f4 Schmid was later to recommend 4.Nc3, with the following possible continuation: 4...a6 5.a4 e6 6.dxe6 Bxe6 7.Bf4 Nc6 8.Nf3 (Or 8.Nge2)

8...Qc7 9.Qd2 Nf6 10.Rd1 O-O-O or 9.Nd5 Bxd5 10.Qxd5 O-O-O, and if 11.Ng5 Rd7! **4...Bg7 5.Nf3 e6 6.dxe6** 6.Nc3, maintaining the tension, is also possible: 6...a6 7.a4 Ne7 8.Be2 exd5 9.exd5 O-O and Black stands well; the exchange 9.Nxd5 Nxd5 10.exd5 only amounts to further harmless simplification, but 9.Nxd5 Nxd5 10.Qxd5?! is effectively answered by 10...Nc6, and if 11.c3 Ne7! **6...fxe6?!** 6...Bxe6, made possible by an early ...d6, was better and more thematic, because 7.c4 would permit Black to use the d4-square and 7.Ng5 could be effectively answered by 7...Ne7, with superior development. 6...fxe6 permits White's next, a sharp pawn thrust which compels Black to close the position. **7.e5! d5** Virtually forced. Black appears to have good control of the center but the development of both of his bishops is hindered. **8.c4 Ne7** Black supports d5 and avoids 8...d4?, a positional error which would allow White to play a knight to e4. **9.Nc3 a6** A multipurpose defensive move. Black prevents Nc3-b5-d6 while threatening queenside expansion by a later ...Rb8 and ...b5; the tactical (but positionally risky) ...dxc4 and ...b5 is also made possible. **10.Bd3?** 10.Be2 was more circumspect, since on d3 the bishop may be harrassed by a later ...Nc6-b4; furthermore, White's pressure on d5 is decreased. A wild possibility was 10.h4!?, to be followed by h5, attempting to exploit the somewhat shaky situation on Black's king-side. **10...Nbc6 11.O-O O-O 12.a3** As noted on move 10, White is forced to waste time preventing 12...Nb4 13.Be2? (Better 13.Bb1) 13...d4! and 14...d3, although White may now consider queen-side expansion with b2-b4. **12...Rb8** However, Black obtains queen-side play first. **13.Rb1 b5 14.cxb5 axb5 15.Bxb5** 15.Nxb5?? c4! **15...d4! 16.Bxc6** The real point of 13.Rb1 is now revealed: If the White rook still resided at a1, Black would win a piece with 16...dxc3, threatening 17...cxb2 as well as 17...Nxc6. Nevertheless, Black will have excellent compensation for his sacrificed pawn: strong control of the center, a good square for his queen at d5, and the possibility ...Bc8-a6. **16...Nxc6 17.Ne4 Qd5 18.Nd6 Ba6**

(See diagram on the next page)

Black highlights the dubious value of White's 'strong' outpost at d6. **19.Re1** If 19.Rf2 instead, Black breaks open the game with 19...g5! 20.Nxg5 (20.fxg5? Nxe5 and the Nd6 is doomed.) 20...Nxe5! 21.fxe5 (21.Qh5? Bd3!) 21...Rxf2 22.Kxf2 Rf8+ 23.Kg1 Bxe5 24.Nde4 Rf1+ 25.Qxf1 Bxf1 26.Kxf1 h6 and the knight still falls. **19...c4** Black must not get carried away with the hyper-fianchettoing of his bishops: 19...Bh6? runs into 20.f5! Bxc1 21.Qxc1 exf5 22.Qh6, and if now 22...Nxe5? 23.Ng5! is crushing.) **20.Nd2?** (A solution based on a tactical misunderstanding, as Black's 21st move will demonstrate. After this, White's game goes rapidly downhill. 20.Qa4 was the best try, although after 20...Rb6 21.Bd2 (trying to get his pieces to breathe) Black has a pleasant choice between 21...Bh6 and 21...Ra8. **20...Rxf4 21.Nd2xc4 Rff8** Now both White knights are threatened. **22.Qa4** 22.b3? Nxc5 **22...Bxc4 23.Nxc4** And not 23.Qxc4 Bxe5 24.Qxd5 exd5, and the knight is again trapped. **23...Ra8** Or simply 23...Nxe5; the text, however, is more forceful. **24.Qc2 d3 25.Qc3 Nd4 26.Bd2** 26.Nb6 is very tempting but bad: 26...Ne2+! 27.Rxe2 dxe2 28.Bd2 Qe5! intending ...Bxe5. **26...Ne2+ 27.Rxe2 dxe2 28.Re1 Qe4 29.b3** 29.Nd6? Rf1+ 30.Rxf1 exf1(Q)+ 31.Kxf1 Rf8+ 32.Kg1 Qe7! **29...Rad8 30.Qe3 Qxe3+ 31.Bxe3 Rd1 32.Bf2 Rxe1+ 33.Bxe1 Rf1** Mate.

Game 5: Bergsma-Diemer, Arnhem 1957

  1.e4 e6 2.d4 c5 3.Nf3 Offering a normal Sicilian... **3...g6** ...which Black declines. Another way of avoiding well-trodden paths was seen in Game 46: Prokopp=Stummer,

Correspondence 1960: 3...b6 4.Nc3 d6 5.Bb5+ Bd7 6.O-O a6 7.Bxd7+ Nxd7 8.Be3 Ngf6 9.h3 Qc7 10.Nd2 Be7 11.Qf3 O-O 12.d5 exd5 13.exd5 b5 and Black had equalized. **4.Nc3 a6**

5.dxc5 White can't stand it any longer and makes this exchange, which forces Black to recapture with his Bf8 and abandon any plans of a king-side fianchetto. **5...Bxc5 6.Be2 b5 7.O-O Bb7 8.e5 Qc7 9.Bf4 f5** Gripping e4 and preventing a White knight from settling there. **10.Qd2 h6 11.h4** White is faced with a dilemma: without 11.h4, Black's king-side pawns roll on unchecked; now, however, White's king-side is weakened and Black obtains a sacrificial lever. **11...Nc6 12.Rfd1 Rd8 13.a3** 13.h5, keeping the h-file closed, might have been a better chance. **13...g5!? 14.hxg5 hxg5 15.Nxg5** Against 15.Bxg5, Diemer had prepared 15...Nxe5 16.Bxd8? Ng4! 17.Bxc7? Bxf2+ 18.Kf1 Rh1+ 19.Ng1 Rxg1 mate; if 17.Rf1 Qg3! with the plan of 18...Bxf3, 19...Qh2 mate. **15...Nxe5 16.Nxe6 Qc6 17.Qd5 dxe6! 18.Qxd8+ Kf7 19.Nd5** If 19.Bf1, then 19...Nf3+! 20.gxf3

Rh1+!! (The marvelous tactical point. 20...Qxf3?? is refuted by 21.Rd7+!, and if 21...Ne7 22.Rxe7+ and 23.Qxh8) 21.Kxh1 Qxf3+ 22.Kh2 Qxf2+ 23.Kh3 Qf3+ 24.Kh2 Qxf4+ 25.Kh3 Qg4+ 26.Kh2 Bg1mate! **19...Ng6 20.Bf3 Nh4 21.Qc7+ Ne7 22.Qxc6 Nxf3+ 23.Kf1** If now 23.gxf3, Black has 23...Bxc6 24.Nxe7 Bxf3! **23...Bxc6 24.Nxe7 Bxe7 25.gxf3 Bxf3 26.Ke1 e5! 27.Bxe5 Rh1+ 28.Kd2 Bg5+ 29.Kc3 Rxd1** White Resigns.

Diemer also employed the Barcza-Larsen-Gunderam concept against 1.d4/2.c4 in the following game:

Game 6: Van Mindeno-Diemer, Beverwijk 1957

1.d4 e6 2.c4 c5 3.d5 Game 6A, Gromotka-Stummer, Correspondence 1960 saw 3.Nf3 b6 4.d5 d6 5.e4 g6 6.Nc3 Bg7 7.Bd2 Ne7 8.Bd3 O-O 9.O-O exd5 10.cxd5 a6 11.h3 b5 12.a3 Nd7 13.Re1 Nf6 14.e5 Nfxd5 15.exd6 Qxd6 16.Ne4 Qc7 17.Rc1 c4 18.b3 c3 19.b4 cxd2 20.Qxd2 Qa7 21.Nc5 Bb7 22.Nxb7 Qxb7 23.Be4 Rad8 24.Nh2 Qa7 25.Ng4 Nb6 26.Nh6+ Bxh6 27.Qxh6 Nc4 28.Qf4 Nd5 29.Qg5 Ndb6 30.Bf3 Rfe8 31.Bc6 Rxe1+ 32.Rxe1 Rf8 33.Qf6 Qb8 34.h4 Qd6 35.Qxd6 Nxd6 36.g3 Ndc4 37.Bb7 Nxa3 38.Bxa6 Rb8 39.Kg2 Nd5 40.Re4 Nc7 and White Resigned. **3...g6 4.Nc3 Bg7 5.Ne4** Here, 5.e4 would transpose into the Gunderam system; instead, White innovates, intent on displacing the Black king. This maneuver, however, costs time, and Black is able to use the additional tempi to further his development. **5...Na6** Encouraging the coming check on d6. **6.Nd6+ Ke7 7.Bg5+ f6 8.Bf4 e5 9.Nxc8+ Rxc8 10.Bd2**

Time to take stock: White has denied Black's king the right to castle and has established a strong pawn at d5, but Black stands better, because of his superior development and central control. **10...Nh6!** A very good move, despite the fact it's the only possible move for this piece. Why? Because Black is thinking about more than just mere development. He envisions the maneuver ...Nh6-f7-d6, positioning his knight on a strong square (ironically, the same one - d6 - that White prematurely occupied) from which it will influence much of the center. **11.e4** White ensures the route ...Nf5-d4 remains closed. **11...Nf7 12.Qa4 Nd6** A position that somewhat resembles Stefan Bucker's Geier (Vulture) system (1.d4 c5 2.d5 Nf6 3.c4 Ne4 with a subsequent ...Nd6) has arisen. **13.Ba5** This just drives Black's queen where it wants to go. **13...Qf8 14.Bd3 f5 15.exf5 e4 16.O-O-O!?** Offering a sacrifice which Black wisely declines. If now 16...exd3? 17.Re1+ Kf7 18.Qxd7+ **16...b5 17.cxb5 c4** An echo of Black's king-side pawn break with 14...f5 15.exf5 e4 **18.Bxe4 Nc5 19.Qc2 Ndxe4** 19...Nb3+?! 20.Kb1 Nxa5 was unclear. **20.Kb1 Qxf5 21.g4!? Qxf2! 22.d6+ Ke8 23.Ne2 c3 24.bxc3 Rf8 25.Rde1** If 25.Rdf1?, Black happily plays 25...Qxf1+! **25...Rf6! 26.Bb4 Re6** Black unhurriedly consolidates his extra piece advantage. **27.Rhf1 Qxh2 28.Rh1 Qf2 29.Ref1 Qe3 30.Re1 Nd2+ 31.Ka1 Nd3 32.Rd1 Nxb4 33.Qxd2 Qxe2 34.Qxe2 Rxe2 35.Kb1 Bxc3 White Resigns.**

Game 7: Gerner-Adam, Switzerland 1958

1.d4 c5 2.d5 d6 3.e4 g6 4.f4 Bg7 5.Nf3 e6 The same position as in Van Scheltinga-Schmid (Game 4), has arisen, but now White goes his own way. **6.Bb5+ Bd7 7.Bxd7+ Qxd7** An unusual recapture, but Black wants to keep an eye on the f5-square, and he has other ideas for developing the Nb8. **8.O-O exd5 9.exd5 Ne7 10.Re1 O-O 11.Nc3 Na6 12.Ne4 Rad8 13.a4 Nb4 14.c4 Nf5 15.Rb1 Rfe8 16.b3 Nd4 17.Nxd4** Forced, else Black will permanently establish a knight on d4. **17...Bxd4+ 18.Kf1 Qf5!**

(See the diagram on the next page)

What's the big deal? White will just play 19.g4 and the Black queen will have to move, right? **19.g4 Qxe4!!** Right!

24

20.Rxe4 Rxe4 21.Bd2 Rde8 Black's sacrifice may now be accurately assessed: he has iron control of the e-file, more active pieces, and, most important, he has forced White into a fatally passive situation. Black has all the play, and will be able to exploit the looseness of White's position. **22.g5 a5 23.Qg4 Nc2 24.Rc1 Ne3+** Black misses an even quicker win with 24...Re1+! 25.Bxe1 Ne3+ **25.Bxe3 Rxe3 26.Rd1 b6 27.Rb1 Re8e4 28.Rd1 Kg7 29.h4 Be5! 30.Kf2 Rxf4+ 31.Qxf4 Bxf4** White Resigns.

Game 8: Noblesse-Duthilleul, Normandy 1958

1.e4 e6 2.d4 c5 3.d5 In Tonka/Duthilleul, Corresp. 1958, White tried to transpose into a Sicilian with 3.Nf3, but after 3...g6 4.Nc3 a6 played 5.d5 anyway. Black gained a good position following 5...d6 6.a4 Bg7 7.Bc4 Nf6 8.Qe2 O-O 9.Bg5 Qa5 **3...g6 4.c4 d6 5.Bd2?!**
(Diagram)

An artificial way of countering Black's ...Bf8-g7. Black

can simply avoid the exchange of dark-squared bishops. **5...Bg7 6.Bc3 Nf6 7.Bd3 O-O 8.Ne2 exd5 9.exd5 b5!** This flank advance is made possible by the hidden weakness in White's position - b2. If now 10.Bxf6 Bxf6 forces White to defend b2. **10.cxb5 Re8** But there's no hurry in regaining material. Black will be able to develop his pieces and target the d5-pawn at his leisure. **11.f3 Bb7 12.Bc4 Nbd7 13.O-O Nb6 14.b3 Nbxd5 15.Bxd5 Bxd5 16.Nd2 Qe7 17.Re1 Qe3+ 18.Kh1 Ng4! 19.fxg4 Qf2 20.Nf3 Bxf3 21.gxf3 Qxf3+ 22.Kg1 Bxc3** and Black won.

Game 9: Lott=Gunderam, Freiburg-Rastatt 1958

1.e4 e6 2.d4 c5 3.d5 g6 3...d6 is a more cautious choice, since it prevents the adventurous 4.d6!? and prepares to meet dxe6 with ...Bxe6 **4.Nf3 d6 5.Nc3 Bg7?!** 5...a6 is better. **6.Bb5+ Bd7 7.Bxd7+** But not 7.dxe6? because of 7...Bxc3+ **7...Qxd7 8.a4 e5 9.O-O Ne7 10.Nd2!** White prepares to place this knight on its best available square, c4, where it will eye the weak d6-pawn and not hinder the pawn advance f2-f4. **10...O-O 11.Nc4 f5 12.f4 Na6 13.fxe5 dxe5 14.Bg5 Nb4 15.d6!?** (Diagram)

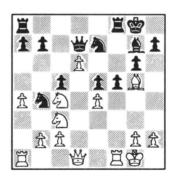

White wants to make use of the d5-square, but this advance is double-edged; the far-flung pawn may become overextended. **15...Nec6 16.Nd5 fxe4 17.Qd2 Qe6 18.Nce3 Nxd5 19.Nxd5 e3** 19...Qxd6?? **20.Ne7+! 20.Nc7 Rxf1+ 21.Rxf1 exd2 22.Nxe6 h6 23.Bxd2 b6 24.d7 Nd8 25.Nxg7 Kxg7 26.Bc3 Nf7 27.Rd1 Rd8** and White eventually struggled to a Draw. The d7-pawn is lost, and the pawn break 28.b4?! is met simply by 28...cxb4.

Game 10: Kruger-Hottes, Landau 1958

1.d4 c5 2.d5 g6 3.e4 Bg7 4.Bd3 d6 5.Ne2 e6 Reaching a Gunderam-type position. **6.O-O Ne7 7.Nec3 O-O 8.a4 Na6 9.Bxa6 bxa6 10.a5** Preventing ...a5 and ...Ba6 **10...Rb8 11.Ra2 exd5 12.Nxd5 Nxd5 13.exd5** And now, a simplified Barcza-Larsen pawn structure appears. **13...Re8 14.Nc3 Bf5 15.Be3 Qh4 16.Qe2 Rb4** Preparing a rook lift to the king-side. **17.Rc1 Rg4 18.g3 Bd4! 19.Nd1 Qh3 20.c3** (Diagram)

20...Rh4! 21.gxh4 Be4 22.f4 Bf3 23.Qf1 Rxe3! With the hideous threat: 24.Qxh3? Re1 mate. **24.Nf2 Re1!** and White Resigns, since mate commencing with 25...Qg4+ is now unavoidable.

Game 11: Clouch-Szekely, Correspondence 1961-62

1.e4 c5 2.d4 e6 Yet another transpositional path! Although the eminent Smith-Morra theorist, GM Janos Flesch, held this move in low regard (recommending 3.d5 with a 'healthy space advantage'), as we have seen, things are not so simple. **3.d5 g6 4.Nf3 Bg7 5.g3** (A rather slow plan of action for White. Again, 5.d6!? may be the most testing try... **5...d6 6.Bg2 Ne7 7.O-O O-O 8.Nc3 a6 9.a4 b6 10.Nd2 exd5 11.exd5 Nd7 12.Nde4 Ne5 13.Be3 h6 14.h3 Nf5 15.Qe2 Nxe3 16.fxe3?** An unnecessary devaluation of White's pawn structure. 16.Qxe3 was natural and best. **16...f5 17.Nd2 Ra7!** The rook lift ...Ra8-a7-f7 is reminiscent of White's play in the Samisch variation of the Nimzo-Indian defense, where the second rank is cleared to permit Ra1-a2-f2. **18.e4 Qg5 19.exf5?**

This exchange is faulty. White sees that his g3-square is weak, but thinks that Black must recapture on f5 with a piece, giving White time to play a knight to e4, defending g3 and hitting the Black queen. **19...gxf5!** Black demonstrates greater flexibility in thought. Since g3 is the target square, opening the g-file so as to play ...Ra7-g7 (and, possibly, ...Rf8-g8) is of great importance. To make this possible, Black will play ...Bg7-e5 (after moving the Ne5) putting even more pressure on the weak g3-pawn. A good example of lazy analysis: tactical surprises are often encountered when one thinks his or her opponent simply 'must' make a certain move, and other possibilities go unanalyzed. **20.Kh2 h5!** A good preparatory move that 'fixes' the g3-pawn and threatens a later ...h5-h4 after Black has played ...Bg7-e5. **21.Nf3 Nxf3+ 22.Qxf3 Be5 23.Ne2 h4 24.Rg1 hxg3+ 25.Nxg3** The knight enters into a deadly pin, but the meek 25.Kh1 constitutes capitulation. **25...Rg7 26.Bh1** White had based all of his defensive hopes on this move. Black's quiet reply is like a sudden, cold shower. **26...Qh4!** White Resigns. Because after 27.Ra3 comes 27...f4! 28.Ne2 Rg3!, and now White cannot defend his h3-square: 29.Nxg3? Qxh3mate; 29.Rxg3+ fxg3+; 29.Qf1 Bxh3! with mate in five moves.

Game 12: Schulz+Grossmann, Correspondence 1975

1.d4 c5 2.d5 e6 Of 2...e6, Gelenczei wrote: "...a two-edged weapon which needs to be handled with great care." **3.e4 g6 4.c4 Bg7 5.f4** White constructs a big pawn center and intends to use it to cramp Black's position. **5...exd5 6.cxd5** Although we will see many examples of exd5 for White, this

28

way of recapturing is definitely best here, since White (having already played 5.f4) wants to play e4-e5 at some time. The c4-square is simultaneously freed for a White piece. **6...d6 7.Nc3 Ne7** With 7...Nf6, Black could transpose into the Modern Benoni, Four Pawns Attack. His Barcza-Larsen move-order gives him the option of playing the knight to e7, as in the game. The principal drawback of 7...Ne7 is that Black cannot put any pressure on White's e4-pawn (as in the Modern Benoni) with moves like ...Nf6 and ...Re8. **8.Nf3 Nd7** In view of what occurs, 8...Bg4, intending ...Nd7 and ...f5, might be better, or 8...a6 9.a4 b6 10.Bd3 Bb7 and only now ...Nd7 **9.Bd3 O-O 10.O-O f5?**
(Diagram)

A positional lemon. Black weakens his e6-square, and is thereby forced to move his Nd7, relinquishing control over e5. **11.Ng5 Nf6 12.e5** White's e5 break, so typical of Modern Benoni positions, is equally effective here. **12...dxe5 13.fxe5 Ne8 14.Bc4 Kh8 15.Bf4 h6 16.Nf3 Ng8** Black is positionally crushed, and with White's next move is deprived of his only remaining try for activity (and a dubious try at that), 17...g5 **17.h4 Nc7 18.a4 Re8 19.Re1 b6 20.Qd3 a5 21.e6** Black Resigns. Korchnoi once likened connected passed pawns to Russian tanks.

Game 13: Armas-Sariego, Manzanillo 1987

1.d4 c5 2.d5 g6 3.c4 d6 4.Nc3 Bg7 5.e4 e6 6.Nf3 If 6.f4, Black can still continue in Gunderam fashion with 6...Ne7, e.g., 7.Nf3 O-O 8.Bd3 f5!? attempting to exploit the broad center. **6...Ne7 7.Be2** Since ...d6 has already been played,

Black can answer 7.dxe6 with 7...Bxe6, and the immediate attack on the d6-pawn by 8.Bf4?! is effectively met by 8...Qa5! Should White try the alternate attack 8.Nb5, Black has 8...Nc8 9.Bf4 O-O, for if 10.Nxd6, then 10...Nxd6 11.Bxd6 Bxb2 **7...O-O 8.O-O a6 9.a4 exd5 10.cxd5 Bg4** 10...h6 11.Nd2 Nd7 12.Nc4 Nb6 13.Na3 Nd7 14.Nc4 Nb6 15.f4 Bd4+ 16.Kh1 Kh7 17.f5 Nxc4 18.Bxc4 g5 19.Bxg5 hxg5 20.Qh5+ Kg7 21.Qxg5+ Ng6 22.Qxd8 Rxd8 23.fxg6 fxg6 and the two bishops left Black with adequate compensation for the sacrificed pawn in Moran/Armas, Manzanillo 1987. **11.Bf4 Nc8** (Diagram)

Black's flexible move order, which enabled him to initially develop his knight at e7, now permits that piece to swing back uniquely to c8, so as to defend the d6-pawn. **12.h3** A more thematic plan, consistent with the pawn structure, would have been 12.Nd2 Bxe2 13.Qxe2 Nd7 14.Nc4 (Using the vacant square) 14...Qe7 15.Rac1 Ne5 16.Nxe5 Bxe5 17.Bxe5 Qxe5 18.f4, and White has an advantage in space. **12...Bxf3** Black gladly exchanges his 'bad' bishop for White's knight. **13.Bxf3 Nd7 14.Qd2 Re8** Black must direct all his energy toward preventing e4-e5. **15.Rab1 Qa5 16.Bg4 Ndb6** 16...Ne5 was simpler. **17.Qd3 Qb4** Tactical restraint of e4-e5 motivated by White's unprotected Bf4. **18.Rfe1 h5 19.Bxc8 Nxc8 20.Qg3 c4** Grimly defending the d6-pawn. **21.a5!?** A pawn sacrifice designed to implement e4-e5. If 21.e5, 21...dxe5 22.Bxe5 Bxe5 23.Rxe5 Rxe5 24.Qxe5 Nd6! gives Black a slight edge. The nice blockading move stops the passed pawn, defends Black's pawns on b7 and c4, and prepares ...Re8. **21...Qxa5 22.e5!** White spurns the pedestrian 22.Bxd6 because of 22...Nxd6 23.Qxd6 Be5! 24.Qd7 b5 **22...h4** A counter-sacri-

30

fice that momentarily diverts the White onslaught. **23.Qxh4 dxe5 24.Ne4 Ne7** Forced, in view of 24...exf4?? 25.Nf6+! **25.Nd6 Nxd5!** And this handy exchange sacrifice completely kills White's momentum. **26.Nxe8 Rxe8** The other plan was 26...Nxf4!? 27.Nf6+ Bxf6 28.Qxf6 Re8 29.Rbd1, with an unclear position. **27.Bg3 b5 28.Rbd1 Bf6 29.Qh6 e4** The Nd5 hangs by a tactical thread: 30.Rxd5?? Qxe1+ **30.Re2 c3!** Deciding matters. The resulting passed pawn is worth far more than the knight invested. **31.Rxd5 Qa1+ 32.Kh2 cxb2 33.Rxb2 Qxb2 34.h4 Bg7 35.Qf4 Qf6 36.Qd2 Qc3 37.Qa2 Qc4 38.Qd2 b4 39.h5 b3** White Resigns.

1B: Black plays ...Nf6/...d6

1B1: White plays g3

Game 14: Evans=Schmid, Helsinki Olympiad 1952

1.d4 c5 2.d5 d6 Again, the Schmid approach to the Benoni (See Game 4); in this game, however, he refrains from his customary fianchettoing by ...g6 and ...Bg7, reaching an opening structure more in line with the Barcza-Larsen system. **3.g3 e5** This move has much the same result as 3...e6 (The normal Barcza-Larsen approach) when White answers as in the present game **4.dxe6 fxe6 5.Bg2 Nf6 6.e4 Nc6 7.Ne2 Be7 8.O-O Rb8 9.h3 O-O 10.Nf4 Bd7 11.Nc3 b5** A good point to begin the queen-side play initiated by 8...Rb8, since White has finally committed his knight to c3. **12.a3 Qc8** Black threatens 13...e5 and 14...Bxh3 **13.Kh2 Nd4 14.Nfe2 Nxe2 15.Nxe2 Bc6 16.f3** The most solid defense in view of Black's potential ...Qb7 **16...d5**
Diagram)

31

With this move, Black has clearly assumed the initiative; the isolated e-pawn he thereby incurs is of little consequence. Evans, however, defends well and is eventually rewarded with the half-point. **17.exd5 Nxd5 18.Qe1 Bd6 19.Bd2 Rb7** Preparing to pile on the pressure with ...Rbf7 **20.Nc3 Nf6 21.Rd1 b4 22.axb4 cxb4 23.Ne2 e5 24.Be3 Nd5 25.Bg1 Rbf7 26.Nc1** The start of a long maneuver resulting in the knight being posted on the strong blockading square e4. **26...Qc7 27.Nb3 Bb7 28.c3 bxc3 29.bxc3 a5 30.Rc1 Nb6 31.Nd2 Nc4 32.Ne4 Bxe4 33.fxe4 Bc5 34.Rxf7 Rxf7 35.h4!** Letting the Bg2 breathe. **35...a4 36.Bh3 Rf6 37.Qe2 Bxg1+ 38.Rxg1 Rb6 39.Kh1 a3** The passed pawn looks ominous, but White jettisons his queenside pawns in exchange for the passer, aided by a pin along the a2-g8 diagonal. **40.Qa2 Qc6 41.Bf1 Qxe4+ 42.Bg2 Qd3 43.Bf1 Qd5+ 44.Rg2 Rc6 45.Bxc4 Qxc4 46.Qxa3 Qxc3 47.Qxc3 Rxc3 48.Re2** White seeks refuge in the pawn-down rook ending, comforted by the inability of Black's king to support the passed e-pawn. **48...Rc5 49.Rf2 Rc6 50.Rf5 Re6 51.Kg2 g6 52.Rf1 Kg7 53.g4 Re7 54.g5 h6 55.Kg3 Ra7 56.Rf6 Re7 57.Rf1 hxg5 58.hxg5 Rf7 59.Re1 Rf5 60.Kg4 Kf7 61.Re4** Draw.

Game 15: Panno+Barcza, Munich Olympiad 1958

1.d4 c5 2.d5 e6 3.Nc3 Nf6 4.g3 d6 5.Bg2 Be7 6.dxe6 fxe6 7.e4 Nc6 8.Nge2 O-O 9.O-O So far, identical to Evans-Schmid; but Barcza now goes his own way **9...Ne8 10.a4 Nc7** An unusual maneuver that aims to support (when possible) the potential pawn advance ...d5 without allowing White to play (after, say, f4) the disruptive move e5. White's heavy pressure on the d5-square and the exchanging threat posed by his next move, however, make Black's plan problematic at best. **11.Nb5!** a6 11...Nxb5? 12.axb5 and White exerts unpleasant pressure along the a-file **12.Nxc7 Qxc7 13.Nf4 Bd7 14.Be3 Rae8 15.c3 Ne5** Here, Black should have played 15...b5! 16.axb5 axb5 intending ...Ra8 with control of the a-file. **16.b3 Rf7** Again, ...b5 came into consideration. **17.Nd3 Ng6** Passive. 17...Nxd3 18.Qxd3 Bc6 was more active; the d6 pawn is defended adequately. **18.b4! cxb4 19.cxb4 Rc8 20.Rc1 Qd8 21.Qb3 Rxc1** Black abandons the c-file in order to defend e6 against Bh3 and Nf4; meanwhile Black eyes a4 and b5. **22.Rxc1 Qe8 23.b5 Nf8 24.Rc7 axb5 25.axb5 Bxb5 26.Rxb7**

26... B xd3 27. Qxd3 Qa8 32 28. Qb1 Qa5

in a worsening position, removing his queen from the latent threat posed by the Bg2: 28...Bf6? 29.e5! Bxe5 30.Rxf7 +- 29.Rb5 Qc3 30.Bh3 Bf6 31.Rb8 Re7 31...Qc4!?, pressuring the e4-pawn and defending e6, was better. 32.Qb6 Kf7 The king, sensing imminent disaster along the back rank, prepares to flee. 33.Qd8 33.Qxd6? Be5! 33...Nd7 34.Qg8+ Kg6

A rather exposed position for the Black monarch, but with the Rb8 under fire, just how is White to continue the attack? 35.Bxe6!! A shattering blow that underlines Black's fatal light-squared weaknesses. 35...Bg5 There is nothing better: 35...Nxb8 36.Bf5+ Kh5 37.Qxh7mate; 35...Rxe6 36.Qxe6 Nxb8 37.Qe8mate. 36.Bf5+ Kf6 37.Rf8+! Nxf8 38.Qxf8+ Ke5 39.f4+ Black Resigns.

1B2: Black plays ...e5?!

Game 16: Stadler=Ljiljak, USSR-Yugoslavia, Budva 1967

1.d4 Nf6 2.Nc3 c5 3.d5 e6 4.e4 d6 5.Nf3 A transposition from the Veresov System 5...e5?! 6.Be2 g6 7.a4 b6 8.Nd2 Be7 9.a5 bxa5 10.Nc4 Ba6 11.Nxa5 Bxe2 12.Qxe2 O-O 13.O-O Qd7 14.h3 Draw. Not much happened here. White found a much more convincing plan against the center-locking ...e5 in Game 19: Ranniku+Grinfeld, Riga 1975.

1B3: White plays Bb5+

Game 17: Szabo+Guimard, Mar del Plata 1962

1.d4 e6 2.Nc3 c5 3.d5 Nf6 4.e4 d6 5.Bb5+ Nbd7
5...Bd7 6.dxe6 fxe6 does not stop 7.e5!?, but after 7...dxe5
8.Nf3, Black is at least afforded the option of 8...Nc6. Roiz-
man/Kikiani, Minsk 1962 saw a different plan for Black after
5...Bd7 6.dxe6 fxe6 7.e5. Here Black played 7...Bxb5, and
after 8.Nxb5 Qa5+ 9.Nc3 dxe5 10.Nf3 Nc6 was only a little
worse. **6.dxe6 fxe6 7.e5! dxe5 8.Nf3 a6 9.Bc4 Nb6 10.Qxd8+
Kxd8 11.Nxe5! Bd6?!** 11...Nfd7!?, directly challenging the Ne5
while preserving the Bf8, was better. The text is based on the
'sacrifice' of the exchange by 12.Nf7+ Ke7 13.Nxh8? Nxc4;
White, however, has no intention of stranding his knight.
12.Nf7+ Ke7 13.Nxd6 Kxd6 14.Bd3 Nbd5 15.Ne4+! Nxe4
after 15...Kc6 16.c4 Nb4, White plays the simple retreat
17.Bb1, with the dual threats of a3 and Be3 **16.Bxe4 Bd7?!**
16...Nf6!?, hoping for 17.Bf3 e5 would have at least attempted
to make something of Black's main liability - the e6-pawn.
17.c4! Ke5

A risky excursion, but the regrouping idea 17...Nb4?!
18.O-O Nc6 runs into 19.Rd1+ Kc7 20.Bf4+, and if 20...e5?
21.Bxc6! wins easily. **18.f3** 18.Bf3? Nb4! **18...Nf6 19.Bxb7 Ra7
20.f4+ Kd4** Seeking to restore material equality, the Black
king walks, as if hypnotized, into a mating net. **21.Bf3 Kxc4
22.Be3 Rc8 23.Kf2! Kb5** 23...Nd5!? **24.b4!!** Forcing a decisive line-opening. **24...Kxb4 25.Rhb1+ Kc4** If 25...Ka5, then
26.Bd2+ Ka4 27.Bd1+ Ka3 28.Bc1mate **26.Rb3!** Black

34

Resigns. White's brutal threat of 27.Rc1mate cannot be countered; even the desperate 26...Nd5 is dispatched by 27.Be2mate.

Game 18: Clarke+Basman, Birmingham 1972

1.d4 c5 2.d5 e6 While this game may not disprove Hartston's assertion that 2...e6 'fails to equalize', it does give some idea of the amount of counterplay an inventive defender like Basman can generate. **3.Nc3 Nf6 4.e4 d6 5.Bb5+ Nbd7 6.dxe6 fxe6 7.e5! Nd5!?** Basman attempts to improve on Szabo+Guimard by refraining from 7...dxe5 **8.exd6** 8.Nxd5 exd5 9.Bxd7+ (9.Qxd5?? Qa5+) Bxd7 10.Qxd5 Bc6!; if 11.Qe6+, then 11...Qe7! 12.Qxe7+ Bxe7 wins back the pawn, because if 13.exd6? Bxg2! **8...Nxc3 9.bxc3 Qf6** 9...Qa5 10.Qh5+ g6 11.Qe5 Kf7!?

is murky but Basmaniacal, e.g., 12.Bxd7! Bxd7 (12...Bg7?? 13.Qxe6+ Kf8 14.Qe8mate) 13.Qxh8 Bg7?! (If 13...Re8 14.Qe5) 14.Qxa8 Qxc3+ 15.Kf1! Bb5+ (15...Qxa1 16.Ne2 Bb5? 17.Qxb7+; 16...Bb2 17.Qxb7; 16...Bh6 17.Qxb7) 16.Ne2 Bxe2+ (16...Qc4 17.Qxb7+ Kg8 18.Qf3 Bxa1 19.Qd3!) 17.Kxe2 Qc4+ 18.Kf3! Qd5+ 19.Kg3 and White escapes; but what happens if Black plays 15...Qxc2!? Mate on d1 is a threat, so: 16.Bh6!! Bb5+ (16...Bxa1?? 17.Qf8mate) 17.Ne2 Qxe2+ 18.Kg1 Bxh6 19.Qxb7+ > 20.d7 +- **10.Nf3** 10.Ne2!? **10...a6** 10...Qxc3+ 11.Bd2 Qb2 12.Rb1! +- **11.Be2** A good example of how to maintain the advantage by losing time! The more 'efficient' 11.Bxd7+ allows Black to unravel with 11...Bxd7, and after 12.O-O, Black can first play the defensive move 13...h6!

followed by 14...O-O-O. The simple bishop retreat leaves Black's pieces still entangled. **11...g6?!** Black is understandably concerned about how to develop his Bf8, but this was the last chance to mix things up with 11...Qxc3+!? **12.O-O Bg7 13.Rb1 O-O 14.c4! b6 15.Bg5** Black's queen is now driven from pillar to post as White's pieces rush into the many weak squares. **15...Qf5 16.Bd3 Qg4 17.h3 Qh5 18.Be4 Rb8 19.Be7 Rf4 20.Re1 Bb7 21.Bxb7 Rxb7 22.Qe2! e5** This weakens the light squares, but 22...Qf5 is answered by 23.g4! Qf7 24.Ng5 +- **23.Qd3 Rb8 24.Re4** 24.Qd5+! followed by 25.Ng5 was much better. **24...Rxe4 25.Qxe4 Qf5 26.Qd5+ Qf7 27.Qc6 Qe8 28.Qd5+** Trying to gain a little time on the clock by repeating moves. **28...Kh8** Black refuses to cooperate. **29.Ng5 h6 30.Ne4 Qg8 31.Qxg8+** If 31.Qc6 then 31...Qc8; 31.Qd3!? was reasonable, but White has no reason to avoid the ending. **31...Kxg8 32.a4 a5 33.Kf1 Bf8** Black needs to challenge the White bishop to get at the d6-pawn, but 33...Kf7 was necessary first. **34.Nf6+!** This simplification removes the blockading knight. **34...Nxf6 35.Bxf6 Kf7** If 35...Bxd6 36.Rd1! and Black's game collapses. **36.Bxe5 Ke6 37.Bg3 Kd7** 37...Bxd6? 38.Re1+ Kd7 39.Rd1 +- **38.Rd1 Re8 39.Re1 Rc8 40.Re3 Rd8 41.Bh4 Rc8 42.Be7** Black Resigns.

Game 19: Ranniku+Grinfeld, Riga 1975

1.d4 Nf6 2.Nc3 c5 3.d5 e6 4.e4 d6 5.Nf3 e5?! 6.Bb5+ Nbd7 7.a4 Be7 8.O-O O-O 9.Bd3 Ne8 Treating the position in true Czech Benoni style, although White has refrained from c2-c4. Black envisions ...g6 and ...Ng7 (intending ...f5), combined with ...Kh8 and ...Nf6-g8 to expel a White bishop should it come to h6. This is a slow plan, but Black is counting on the closed center to frustrate any immediate aggression by White. **10.b3** An unusual idea. White often plays (after preparation by Rb1) b4 instead, aiming to dominate the b-file and control the queen-side. **10...Kh8 11.Bb2 g6 12.Nfd2 Ng7 13.Nc4 g5?!** Preventing f2-f4, but the f5 and h5 squares are weakened seriously. **14.Ne2 Nf6 15.Ng3 Bd7 16.Qd2 Rb8 17.Rfe1** 17.Qxg5? Nxe4 **17...b6 18.Rad1 Rb7?**

(See diagram at the top of the next page)

18...Ng8!?, giving Black's pieces some breathing room, would have prevented White's following combination. **19.Nxe5! dxe5 20.Ba6 Qb8 21.d6 Bd8 22.Bxe5** White's eccentric fianchetto becomes meaningful. **22...Ng4 23.Bb2 f6 24.f4 Be6 25.Bxb7 Qxb7 26.h3 Nh6 27.fxg5 fxg5 28.Nh5 Rf7 29.Nxg7 Rxg7 30.Rf1 Kg8 31.Qc3 Qd7 32.Rf2!** Black Resigns. The White mating plan of Rdf1 followed by Rf8 mate can only be stopped by heavy loss of material.

Game 20: Muller-Bonsch, Groditz 1976

1.d4 Nf6 2.Nc3 e6 3.e4 c5 4.d5 d6 5.Bb5+ Bd7 5...Nbd7 is preferable; exchange of bishops normally favors White. **6.a4 e5** Black decides to block the center and give the position a Spanish Benoni flavor. **7.Nge2** White demonstrates an equally flexible mindset, leaving his f-pawn unblocked. **7...g6 8.O-O a6 9.Bxd7+ Nbxd7 10.Ng3 Bg7 11.Ra3 O-O 12.a5 h6** The immediate 12...Nf8 was probably preferable. **13.Qe2 Kh7 14.Nd1** Heading for c4. **14...Ne8 15.Ne3 Nc7 16.c4** White was reluctant to play 16.c3, preventing ...Nc7-b5-d4 while permitting Nc4, but blocking the third rank in the process. **16...Rh8 17.Bd2 Ne8 18.Rb1 h5 19.h3 Nef6 20.Nc2 h4!? 21.Nf1 Bh6** Black seizes the opportunity to exchange off his bad bishop. **22.Bxh6 Kxh6 23.Ne1 Kg7 24.Nd3 b6?!** 24...b5 was better, preventing 25.b4 **25.axb6?** White misses his chance to favorably open the queen-side with 25.b4! **25...Qxb6 26.Nd2 Rhb8 27.Rba1 Ra7 28.Nb3 a5! 29.Nd2** 29.Nxa5? just strands the knight after 29...Rba8 30.Nc6 Rxa3 31.bxa3 Qb3, and 29.Rxa5 is no improvement: 29...Rxa5 30.Nxa5 Ra8 31.Nb3 Rxa1+ 32.Nxa1 Qa6 wins back the pawn with a better

position. **29...Qc7 30.f3?** An unnecessary weakening of g3.
30...Nh5 31.Qe1 Qd8 32.Nf1 Rb4!
(Diagram)

A positional exchange sacrifice. In the closed position
that results, the Black knights are better than the White rooks.
33.Nxb4?! Sometimes, the best way to refute a sacrifice is to
not accept it. Black gains useful squares for his knights.
**33...cxb4 34.Re3 Nf4 35.Qf2 Nc5 36.Kh1 Qg5 37.b3 Ra8
38.Rb1** (38.Ra2 was a better defensive try.) **38...a4 39.bxa4
Rxa4 40.Qd2 b3 41.Rb2 Rxc4 42.Re1 Rd4** White Resigns.
43.Qa5 Ncd3 44.Ree2 Nxb2 45.Rxb2 Rd1

Game 21: Vesely+Zdenek, Czechoslovakia 1981

**1.d4 Nf6 2.Nc3 c5 3.d5 e6 4.e4 d6 5.Bb5+ Nbd7 6.a4
e5** The same plan as in Muller-Bonsch (Game 20); here,
however, Black does not fianchetto. **7.Nf3 Be7 8.O-O O-O
9.Nd2 Rb8 10.Be2 Ne8 11.Nc4 Nb6 12.Ra3! Nxc4 13.Bxc4 f5
14.f4!** Black has played his logical lever, ...f5, but now faces a
central dilemma, since neither pawn capture is attractive:
14...exf4 is met strongly by 15.e5! and 14...fxe4 by 15.fxe5!
Black shied away from 14...Nf6 because of 15.exf5 Bxf5 16.g4!
Bd7 17.g5 Ne7 18.fxe5, settling instead for... **14...Kh8?** Black
removes his king from the dangerous g8-a2 diagonal, but further examination of 14...Nf6 was in order: 15.exf5 could have
been met by 15...exf4!, and if 16.Ne2 Bxf5 **15.exf5 exf4
15...Bxf5?** 16.g4! Bd7 17.f5 > Ne4 +- **16.Ne2 Bxf5 17.Nxf4
Nc7 18.g4! Bd7 19.Rh3 Kg8 20.Qd3 h6**

(See the diagram at the top of the next page)

38

Storm clouds are gathering around Black's king; if 20...g6 21.Nxg6! Even after 20...h6, however, White has a devastating shot. **21.Rxh6! Bf5** Black could not play 21...gxh6: 22.Qg6+ Kh8 23.Qxh6+ Kg8 24.Qg6+ Kh8 25.Bd3! **22.gxf5 gxh6 23.Qg3+ Kh8** 23...Kh7 is also hopeless: 24.Qg6+ Kh8 25.Nh5 Bf6 26.Qxh6+ Kg8 27.Bg5!; 23...Bg5 24.h4 Rxf5 25.Bd3 Re5 26.Ng6! **24.Ng6+** Black Resigns.

Game 22: Alexandria-Levitina, Dubna 1984

1.d4 Nf6 2.Nf3 c5 3.d5 d6 4.Nc3 e6 5.dxe6 White's exchange only eases Black's defensive task. 5.e4 exd5 6.exd5 or 5.Bg5 would have been stronger. **5...Bxe6 6.e4 Be7 7.Bb5+** 7.e5 dxe5 8.Qxd8+ Bxd8 9.Bb5+ Bd7 10.Nxe5 Bxb5 11.Nxb5 O-O leads to nothing for White. **7...Bd7** In this particular position, interposing the bishop is best, since if 7...Nbd7? 8.Ng5! **8.a4 O-O 9.O-O Nc6 10.h3 Nb4** If Black can safely play ...d5 in this variation, she should obtain equal chances. **11.Re1 Bxb5 12.Nxb5 a6 13.Nc3 d5 14.e5!?** White is unwilling to allow simplification by 14.exd5 Nbxd5 15.Nxd5 Nxd5 [15...Qxd5?? 16.Qxd5 Nxd5 17.c4] and tries to maintain some tension in the position. **14...Ne8 15.Ne2 d4 16.Nf4 Nc7 17.c3 Nc6 18.cxd4 cxd4 19.Qb3 Qd7 20.Bd2** Here, and later, White spurns the thematic e5-e6. **20...Ne6** Black takes the opportunity to temporarily blockade the dangerous e-pawn. **21.Nxe6 Qxe6 22.Qd3** The b7-pawn is still poisoned: 22.Qxb7? Rfb8 **22...Rad8 23.Rad1 Rd5 24.Bf4 Rfd8 25.Re4 Qg6 26.Rde1** Black defends the d-pawn tactically: 26.Nxd4? Nxd4 27.Rxd4 Qxd3 **26...a5 27.Qb3 Bb4 28.Bd2 Bxd2 29.Nxd2 Nb4 30.f4** 30.e6!? would have considerably sharpened the fight. **30...Qc6**

31.Nc4?
(Diagram)

Again, 31.e6 was better than this move, which abandons the blockade of Black's d-pawn. **31...d3! 32.Nd6** Now it's too late to recant: 32.Nd2 Nc2 33.Rd1 Qc5+ 34.Kh2 Qf2 **32...d2! 33.Rd1 R5xd6! 34.Rxb4 Rd3** This zwischenzug settles it. **35.Rxd2 Rxd2 36.Rxb7 Qxg2** mate.

Game 23: Nikolic=Ristic, Smederevska Palanka 1984

1.d4 c5 2.d5 Nf6 3.Nc3 d6 4.e4 e6 Reaching, by transposition, the same position as after 1.e4 e6 2.d4 c5 3.d5 Nf6 4.Nc3 d6 **5.Bb5+ Nbd7 6.dxe6 fxe6 7.Nf3 a6 8.Bxd7+** 8.Bc4 Nb6 **8...Nxd7!** Avoiding 8...Bxd7? 9.e5! **9.Ng5!? Ne5 10.f4 Nf7 11.Nxf7 Kxf7 12.O-O**
(Diagram)

Black's king now appears precariously placed, but Ristic smoothly unravels his sleeping pieces and shuttles his monarch

40

to safety. **12...Be7 13.f5 Rf8!** Black is unafraid of the onrushing f-pawn and defends calmly; if 13...exf5? 14.exf5 and Black's king is in trouble, since Qd5+ is threatened. **14.fxe6+ Kg8 15.Bf4** If 15.Rxf8+ Qxf8, followed by ...Qf6, and the e6-pawn falls. **15...Rf6 16.Nd5 Rxe6 17.Nxe7+ Qxe7 18.Qd5 Bd7 19.Qxb7 Qe8 20.Rad1 Bc6 21.Qb3 c4 22.Qc3 Qg6 23.Qxc4 Bxe4 24.Rd2** And the possibility of 24...d5, followed by 25...Rc6 (as well as the bishops of opposite color), prompted the players to agree to a... **Draw.** A short but sharp little game where White kept seeming to get the upper hand, only to encounter a strong defensive reply at each turn.

Game 24: Benjamin+Shaine, U.S. Open (Boston) 1988

1.e4 e6 2.d4 c5 3.d5 d6 3...exd5, leading to the main line Barcza-Larsen, is probably better. **4.Nc3 Nf6 5.Nf3** Benjamin tries to improve on Szabo-Guimard (Game 17), by first playing Nf3 and waiting to see what Black will do. **5...Be7** 5...a6! **6.Bb5+ Bd7** 6...Nbd7? 7.dxe6 dxe6 8.Ng5! **7.dxe6 fxe6 8.e5!**

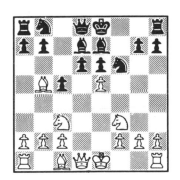

8...dxe5 9.Nxe5 Bxb5 10.Qxd8+ Bxd8 11.Nxb5 O-O 12.Be3 Na6 13.c3 Nd5 14.Bd2 Rf5 15.Nc4 Be7 16.O-O Rd8?! Letting the a-pawn go for nebulous tactical chances. **17.Nxa7 Nac7 18.a4** Now ...Ra8 is no threat. **18...Nf4 19.Nb5 Ncd5 20.Rae1 Nf6 21.g3 Nd3 22.Rxe6 Nxb2 23.Nxb2 Rxd2 24.Nc4 Rd7 25.Nb6** Black Resigns. A game with a clear moral: don't let White play e5, especially in positions where White has the additional option of initiating the exchange dxe6, leaving Black with an isolated e-pawn and a very difficult end-game.

What happens when Black plays as above but omits ...d6, avoiding the annoying Bb5+? There is a trap of which Black must be aware, as in:

Game 25: Smejkal+Savon, Wijk aan Zee 1972

1.d4 c5 2.d5 e6 3.e4 Another transpositional route. Jaenisch (1842!) analyzed the continuation 3...d6 4.c4 Nf6 5.Nc3, and concluded White stood better. **3...Nf6 4.Nc3 exd5?** Black thinks that White has nothing better than 5.exd5 d6, leading into the main line. **5.e5!**

5...Ng8 Abject retreat, but 5...d4 allows the trap to spring shut with 6.exf6 dxc3 7.Qe2+! winning a piece, and if 5...Qe7, then 6.Qe2 Ne4 7.Nxd5 Qxe5 8.Nc3 d5 9.f3 f5 10.fxe4 fxe4 11.Nf3 Qf5 12.Nh4! Resigns, as in Game 25A: Mariotti+Cosulich, Venice 1971 **6.Qxd5** With a clear positional advantage for White. Play continued... **6...Nc6 7.Nf3** 7.Bc4!? **7...d6 8.Bb5 Ne7!?** 8...dxe5? 9.Nxe5! +- **9.Qxd6 Qxd6 10.exd6 Nf5 11.Bf4 Bxd6 12.Bxd6 Nxd6** Restoring material equality, but White now proceeds to shatter Black's queen-side pawns, ensuring an advantageous endgame. **13.Bxc6+ bxc6 14.0-0-0 Nb5 15.Ne4 Bg4 16.Nxc5 0-0** Black unfortunately has no time to mangle White's pawns with 16...Bxf3? because of 17.Rhe1+! +- **17.Rd3** White is now a sound pawn ahead and converts his advantage with excellent technique. **17...Rfe8 18.c4 Bxf3 19.Rxf3 Nd6 20.b3 f6 21.Rd1 Nf7 22.Rfd3 Re5 23.Nb7 Re7 24.Rd7** Seizing the seventh rank and forcing favorable simplification. **24...Kf8 25.Rxe7 Kxe7 26.Nc5 Nd6 27.Re1+ Kf7 28.Re6 Rd8 29.a4 a5 30.Kb2 Nf5 31.Kc3 Nd6 32.Re3 g5**

**33.Rh3 Kg6 34.Rd3 Kf7 35.f3 h5 36.Na6 Ke7 37.c5 Nf5
38.Rxd8 Kxd8 39.b4 axb4+ 40.Nxb4 Kc7 41.Nc2 Nh4 42.Ne1
Kb7 43.Kd4 Nf5+ 44.Ke4 Ne7 45.f4 g4 46.Nd3 Ka6** It's
beginning to look like Black is making progress, since White
cannot prevent ...Ka5. But Smejkal has seen farther than that...
47.Nb4+ Ka5

48.Nxc6!! Nxc6 49.Kd5 Nb4+ 49...Ne7 50.Ke6! **50.Kd6 Na6
51.c6 Kb6** Desperately trying to organize a blockade on c7, but
White has a simple reply. **52.a5+! Ka7** 52...Kxa5 53.c7! Nxc7
54.Kxc7 and Black's pawns fall. **53.f5! Kb8 54.Ke6 Nb4
55.Kxf6 Nxc6 56.Kg7** Black Resigns.

1B4: White plays dxe6 (without Bb5+)

Game 26: Ree+Wirthensohn, Haifa Olympiad 1976

1.e4 e6 2.d4 c5 3.d5 Nf6 4.Nc3 d6 5.dxe6 Bxe6 This is
tempting, as it develops a piece and seems to avoid the cramp
associated with lines where White plays Bb5+; however, even
though ...Nc6 is now possible, White's next move indicates that
5...fxe6 is probably preferable. **6.f4 Nc6** 6...g6?! 7.f5 (Anyway!) 7...gxf5 8.exf5 Bxf5?! 9.Qf3 Qc8 10.Bb5+! Nc6
11.Bxc6+ bxc6 12.Nge2 with compensation for the pawn. **7.f5
Bc8 8.Nf3 Be7 9.Bc4 O-O 10.O-O a6** 10...Ne5!? was a possibility. **11.a4 Nb4** Angling for ...d5 **12.Bf4 b6 13.Qe2 Bb7
14.Rad1 Qc7** Running from the imminent e4-e5, but this move
occurs anyway. **15.e5! Bxf3 16.Rxf3 dxe5 17.Bxe5 Qc6 18.Bg3
Rfe8 19.Re3 Qb7 20.Bh4!** Now Black's king-side pawns will
be ruined. **20...Bf8 21.Bxf6 Rxe3 22.Qxe3 gxf6 23.Ne4 Kh8**

24.Nxf6 Qc6 25.Nh5 Nxc2 26.Qe5+ f6 27.Nxf6 Bg7 28.Rd6 Qc7 29.Qe6 Nd4

30.Rxd4! cxd4 31.Ne8 A rather nasty example of line-interference. **31...Qxc4 32.Qxc4 Rxe8** and Black Resigns.

Game 27: Speelman+Suba, Dortmund I, 1981

1.d4 Nf6 2.Nf3 c5 3.d5 e6 4.Nc3 d6 5.e4 a6?! An ambitious try for immediate queen-side play. 5...exd5 was safer. **6.dxe6 Bxe6** If 6...fxe6, White has the thematic and strong 7.e5! **7.Ng5!** This is more than just an attempt to gain the two bishops; Black also ends up with a very weak pawn on e6. **7...b5 8.Nxe6 fxe6 9.g3!** White shows excellent positional judgment; the bishop will be powerfully placed at g2 (or even h3), where it will be able to exploit Black's weak light squares. **9...Nc6** 9...b4 10.Ne2 Nxe4?! 11.Bg2 d5 12.Nf4 Qf6 13.O-O > Nd5 **10.Bg2 Qc7 11.O-O Be7 12.Ne2 Kf7?!**

While it is easy to criticize such an extravagant defense of the e6-pawn, Black is very limited in his options here; his painful choices were brought about by allowing White to inflict the weakness at e6 in the first place. If 12...O-O, White plays 13.Nf4, and now neither 13...Qc8 14.Bh3 Nd8 15.Nd5! nor 13...Qd7 14.Bh3 Nd8 15.e5! are satisfactory for Black; 12...e5?, keeping the knight out of f4, is positional suicide. White would then be confronted with an embarrassment of riches: Ne2-c3-d5, Bg2-h3, and f2-f4. **13.Nf4 Rhe8?** The wrong rook. White is coming for the head of Black's king, and Black should be concentrating his forces on the king-side to repulse the assault. The bright side of 12...Kf7?! was that it at least connected Black's rooks and permitted 13...Rae8 14.Bh3 Nd8!?, offering better prospects of a satisfactory defense. **14.a4 b4 15.g4! h6 16.h4 g5** 16...Nh7 looks like it does a better job of holding up g4-g5, but there is a tactical flaw: 17.Nxe6! Kxe6 18.Qd5+ Kd7 (18...Kf6?? 19.Qf5 is a picturesque mate) 19.Qf5+, winning back the piece and remaining a pawn ahead. **17.Nh3 Nh7 18.f4 Kg7** The pawn storm is raging, and Black's king can merely run before the blows. If 18...gxh4, White crashes through with 19.g5! **19.hxg5 hxg5 20.fxg5 Ne5** Has the knight found peace within the hurricane's eye? **21.g6!** No! **21...Nxg6 22.Qd2** Now that Black's defenses have been shredded, the second wave - the heavy pieces - prepare to rush in. **22...Nhf8 23.Nf4 Nxf4 24.Qxf4 Bd8 25.e5 d5 26.Qh6+ Kg8 27.Rxf8+!** White simplifies into a winning ending. **27...Rxf8 28.Qxe6+ Qf7** Forced, in view of 28...Kh8 29.Qh6+ Kg8 30.Bxd5+ **29.Qxf7+ Rxf7 30.Bxd5 Rc8 31.Be3 Kg7 32.Bxf7 Kxf7 33.Rf1+ Kg7 34.Kg2 Be7 35.e6 Kg6 36.Rf5 Rc6 37.Re5 Kf6 38.Re4 Rd6** 38...Rxe6? 39.Bg5+! **39.Kf3 Rd1 40.b3 Rd5 41.Bf2 Kg6 42.Ke2 Kg5 43.Bg3 Rd8 44.Kf3 Kg6 45.Rf4 Rd6 46.Rf5 Rd2** 46...Rxe6 47.Re5 Rf6+ 48.Bf4 Bd6 49.Rg5+ Kh7 50.Rf5 **47.Rf7 Bf6 48.Rf8 Rxc2 49.Be5! Be7** 49...Bxe5? 50.e7 **50.Rg8+ Kh6 51.Re8 c4 52.Rxe7** Black Resigns.

Game 28: Vaganian=Suba, Tallinn 1983

1.d4 Nf6 2.Nf3 c5 3.d5 e6 4.Nc3 a6!? Suba is often described as an eternal optimist. Undaunted by a crushing loss against Speelman (Game 27), he persists in seeking rapid queen-side play in this variation. **5.e4 b5 6.e5 b4**

7.dxe6 7.exf6 bxc3 is good for Black. **7...dxe6 8.Qxd8+ Kxd8 9.Nb1 Nd5 10.Nbd2 Nd7 11.g3 h6 12.Bg2 Rb8 13.O-O g5 14.Nc4 Bg7 15.Re1** White's position is slightly better, but Suba defends resourcefully. **15...Ke7 16.h4 gxh4 17.Nxh4 Bb7 18.f4 N5b6 19.Nxb6 Nxb6 20.f5 Kd7 21.Bxb7 Rxb7 22.a3 b3!** A good temporary pawn sacrifice that avoids the opening of the a-file. **23.f6 Bf8 24.Rd1+ Kc6 25.cxb3 Nd5 26.Rd3 Rg8 27.Bd2 Rd7 28.Nf3** If 28.Rf3, 28...Nxf6 anyway. **28...Nxf6 29.Rxd7 Nxd7 30.Bf4 Bg7 31.Rd1 Rb8 32.Rd6+ Kc7 33.Nd2 Nxe5 34.Rxa6 Rd8 35.Ne4 Rd5 36.Ra8 f5 37.Nxc5 Rxc5 38.Ra7+ Kd8 39.Rxg7 Ng4 40.Bd2 Rc2 41.Bc3 e5 42.a4 e4 43.a5 Nh2 44.Bf6+ Kc8 45.Re7** Draw. Black holds the balance with 45...Ng4! 46.Bc3 [46.Bd4 Rc1+ 47.Kg2 Rc2+ 48.Kf1? Nh2+ 49.Ke1 Nf3+ 50.Kd1 Rd2+ > 51...Rxd4] 46...Rc1+ 47.Kg2 Rc2+ 48.Kf1 Ne3+ 49.Ke1 Ng2+ 50.Kd1 Ne3+ 51.Ke1 Ng2+ 52.Kf1 Ne3+ 53.Kg1 Rg2+ 54.Kh1 Rf2!; or 45...Ng4! 46.Re8+ Kc7 47.a6?! (47.Re7+ Kd6; 47.Bd4/47.Bc3 Rc1+ etc.; 47.Be5+?? Kd7) 47...Rc1+ [47...Nxf6? 48.a7] 48.Kg2 Ra1

Game 29: Belke-Pahtz, Berlin 1988

1.d4 Nf6 2.Nf3 c5 3.d5 d6 4.Nc3 e5 5.dxe6 Reaching by transposition the same situation as after 1.d4 c5 2.d5 e6 3.Nc3 Nf6 4.Nf3 d6 5.dxe6 **5...Bxe6 6.e4 Nc6 7.Bg5?!** This is the wrong place for the bishop; a better idea would be 7.Bf4 or, preferably, 7.Ng5 **7...Be7 8.Be2 h6! 9.Bh4** A plausible move, but the bishop is not out of danger here. **9...O-O 10.O-O**

(See the diagram at the top of the next page)

10...Nxe4! Black executes a petite combinaison. **11.Bxe7** After 11.Nxe4 Bxh4 12.Qxd6 (12.Nxh4 Qxh4 13.Nxd6 Rad8!) 12...Be7 Black has a slight advantage.) **11...Nxc3 12.Bxd8 Nxd1 13.Bc7 Nxb2 14.Bxd6 Rfd8 15.Bxc5 Na4!** The last laugh! **16.Ba3** Unfortunate, but after 16.Be3 Nc3 17.Bd3 comes 17...Nb4 (or simply 17...Nxa2), and if 18.Nd4 Nxd3 19.cxd3?, then 19...Rxd4! **16...Nc3! 17.Bd3 a5!** The White bishop-pair is virtually useless. **18.Rfe1 Nb4 19.Bb2 Nbxa2!** Black, with an extra pawn and a superior position, is now winning. **20.Re5 a4 21.Ba3 Rd5! 22.Rxd5 Bxd5 23.Nd4 g6** Preventing 24.Nf5 **24.Re1 Rb8 25.Bd6 Rd8 26.Ba3 Rc8** Black threatens further simplification with 27...Bc4 **27.Re7 Nb1 28.Bd6 Nac3 29.Nb5 Nxb5 30.Bxb5 a3** Runaway train! **31.Be5 Nc3! 32.Re8+ Rxe8 33.Bxe8 Nb1 34.Bb5 a2 35.Bd3 Na3 36.Kf1 Bc6 37.f3 Ba4 38.c4 b6 39.Ke2 Bb3 40.Kd2 Bxc4 41.Bd4 b5 42.Bxc4 Nxc4+ 43.Kc2 Ne3+! 44.Kb3 Nxg2 45.Kxa2 Nh4** White Resigns.

1B5: Unusual Black Plans Prior to 4...exd5:

An example of ...exd5 before White plays e2-e4 was seen in the following game. It is, perhaps, a foreshadowing of the currently popular line 1.d4 Nf6 2.Nf3 c5 3.d5 e6 4.Nc3 exd5 5.Nxd5 Nxd5 6.Qxd5.

Game 30: Vaganian+Quinteros, Biel Interzonal 1985

1.d4 c5 2.d5 e6 3.Nc3 exd5 3...Nf6 4.e4 exd5? 5.e5!; 4...d6 leads to lines considered previously; Quinteros avoids transposition to Szabo+Guimard (Game 17) and

Clarke+Basman (Game 18), but White still gets the upper hand. **4.Nxd5 Ne7 5.Bg5 Qa5+ 6.Bd2 Qd8** There's nothing better, but Black is perfectly willing to repeat moves and draw. **7.Bc3 Nxd5 8.Qxd5 d6 9.e4**

White is doing rather better in this position as compared with analogous Barcza-Larsen lines. For one thing, White has not had to play exd5, and Black's d6-pawn is therefore unshielded and subject to attack down the d-file. Black's development is also lagging, and even if time will be gained attacking the White queen, White will be able to post her on a good square. **9...Nc6 10.Bb5 Qb6 11.Qd3 Be6 12.Ne2** This flexible development is another indication that Black's third move might have been best played after White had committed to Ng1-f3 and e2-e4. **12...a6 13.Bxc6 Qxc6 14.Nf4 O-O-O 15.O-O Re8 16.Rfe1 f6 17.Nxe6 Rxe6 18.Rad1 Be7 19.Qc4 Kd7 20.f4 Bd8 21.f5 Re7 22.e5! fxe5 23.Rxe5 Rhe8 24.Rxe7 Rxe7 25.f6! gxf6 26.Bxf6 Re4 27.Qf7+ Kc8 28.Bxd8 Kxd8 29.Qxh7** White has smoothly transformed his advantages in space and development into a more tangible material plus. **29...Re2 30.Qg7 Qe8** 30...Rxc2? 31.Qg8+! Qe8 (31...K-any 32.Qh7+) 32.Rxd6+ **31.Qg3 Kc8 32.h4** And now White gives back material to start his decisive pawn advance. **32...Rxc2 33.Rxd6 Rxb2 34.Rg6 Kd7 35.Rg7+ Kc6 36.Qf3+ Kd6 37.Qf4+ Kd5 38.Rg5+ Kc6 39.Qf6+ Kc7 40.Rxc5+ Kb8 41.Qe5+ Qxe5 42.Rxe5 Rxa2 43.h5 Ra4 44.g3** A handy little move that prevents Black from getting behind the passed pawn and forces him to defend from in front of the pawns. **44...Rg4 45.Kf2 Rg8 46.h6 Kc7 47.Re7+ Kd6 48.Rg7 Rh8 49.Rg6+ Ke5 50.g4 a5 51.Kg3 a4 52.Kh4 a3 53.Kh5** Reaching the critical square just in time to refute 53...a2? by 54.Rg5+

and 55.Ra5 **53...Kf4 54.Rf6+ Kg3 55.g5 a2 56.Rf1 Ra8
57.Rg1+ Kf3 58.Rf1+ Kg3 59.Ra1 b5 60.g6 b4**

61.g7! Simple but accurate. Predictably, perhaps, the flashy
61.Rxa2? ruins all of White's hard work and only draws:
61...Rxa2 62.g7 Kf4! 63.h7 Kf5 64.Kh4 Kf4 65.Kh3 Ra3+
66.Kh2 Ra2+ 67.Kg1 Ra1+ 68.Kf2 Ra2+ 69.Ke1 Ke3!
70.Kd1 Kd3 71.Kc1 Kc3 72.Kb1 Rb2+ 73.Ka1 Kc2! **61...b3
62.Rg1+ Kf3** 62...Kf2 63.h7 Kxg1 64.g8(Q)+! **63.h7 Ra5+
64.Kh4 Ra4+ 65.Kh3 a1(Q) 66.g8(Q)!** Black Resigns.

This seems like an appropriate place to include a game
that falls somewhere in between Black's attempts to
delay ...exd5 and White's reinforcing try c2-c4 (after a
normal ...exd5). In the following game, Black makes use of an
early ...a6 and ...b5, doing without ...d6 and encouraging White
to play d5-d6 instead!

Game 31: Kidd-Blackmore, British Postal Chess Federation 1987 Open Championship, Best Game Prize

1.e4 e6 2.d4 a6 Temporarily parting company with our
Barcza-Larsen schemes and offering to go into a St. George
Defense. Although White tries to discourage this with 3.c4
(and/or goad Black into making a St. George gambit of it with
3...b5), Black is still able to have things his own way. **3.c4 c5
4.d5 exd5** Here, Black could have accelerated his queen-side
mischief with 4...b5!?, and after 5.Nf3 Nf6 6.Nc3 b4 7.e5
would have transposed into Christiansen-Alburt, US Ch. 1985,
which continued 7...bxc3 8.exf6 Qa5 9.bxc3 gxf6 10.Bd2 f5

49

11.Bd3 Bg7 12.O-O d6 13.Re1 O-O 14.dxe6?! (14.Qc2!) 14...fxe6 15.Ng5 e5 16.Qf3 Ra7 17.Rab1 Qc7!, 0-1, in 48 moves. Benjamin and Schiller, in Unorthodox Openings, state that Black should avoid 8...Qa5 and instead play 8...gxf6, although Ftacnik+Fauland, Vienna 1986, continued 9.Bd3 Bg7 10.O-O f5 11.bxc3 d6? 12.dxe6 fxe6 13.Bxf5! exf5 14.Qd5! with advantage for White. The authors of the unexplored openings further indicate that Klinger's suggested 11...O-O 12.Bg5 Qa5 can be satisfactorily met by 13.Rb1, intending Bg5-e7-d6. The Swedish analyst Martens, however, may have solved Black's problem by discovering 8...cxb2! After 9.Bxb2 gxf6 10.Bd3 Bg7 11.Qc2 O-O! 12.O-O f5! Black is slightly better. **5.exd5** And so, after a rather weird transposition of moves, we arrive at a position that might have developed more 'naturally' by 1.e4 e6 2.d4 c5 3.d5 exd5 4.exd5 a6?! 5.c4 **5...b5!?** **6.d6** A bone in Black's throat or just another overextended pawn? **6...Qf6 7.Nc3 Bb7 8.Qe2+ Qe6 9.Bf4 g5! 10.Qxe6+ dxe6 11.Bxg5 b4 12.Na4 Nd7 13.O-O-O Nh6**

14.f3 14.Bxh6? Bxh6+ 15.Kb1? Be4+ 16.Ka1 Bc2! **14...Nf5 15.b3 Bxd6 16.Bd3 Nd4 17.Ne2 Rg8 18.h4 f6 19.Be3 Rxg2 20.Bxd4** 20.Nxd4 cxd4 21.Bxd4 Bf4+ 22.Kb1 e5 23.Bb2 Bxf3 leaves Black better. **20...Bxf3** 20...cxd4 21.Nxd4 Bf4+ 22.Kb1 e5 23.Ne6! **21.Rhf1 Bxe2 22.Bxe2 Rxe2 23.Bxf6 Nxf6 24.Rxd6 Ke7 25.Rfd1 h5** Or 25...Rxa2 26.Kb1 Rxa4 27.bxa4 Nd5, but White could instead play 26.Nxc5 **26.Nxc5 Rc8 27.Nd3** Not falling into 27.Nxa6? Nd5! and setting a counter-trap. **27...Rxa2** 27...Ne4? 28.Rxe6+! **28.Nxb4 Ra1+ 29.Kb2 Rxd1 30.Rxd1 a5 31.Nd3 a4 32.c5 Rd8 33.b4 Rd4 34.b5 Ne4 35.b6** 35.Re1? a3+! 36.Ka1 Nc3 37.Re3 Rxh4 38.Ne1 Nxb5 and Black wins. **35...Nxc5 36.Nxc5 Rxd1 37.b7 Rd8 38.Na6**

Kf6 39.Nc5 Kf5 40.Ka3 Rb8 41.Kxa4 Kg4 42.Kb5 Kxh4 43.Kb6 Kg4 44.Nxe6 h4 White Resigns.

Chapter 2: White alternatives on move 5 after 1.e4 e6 2.d4 c5 3.d5 exd5 4.exd5 d6

We now consider the variations leading to the 'main line' Barcza-Larsen; namely, those where Black implements the exchange ...exd5 when White has already played e2-e4 and is constrained to recapture by exd5. Most games that follow employ the 'traditional' move order 1.e4 e6 2.d4 c5 3.d5 exd5 4.exd5 d6 (or transpose rapidly). There are, however, a few examples featuring an early ...Nf6 by Black; these also subsequently transpose into the lines we will now examine.

2A: White plays 5.c4

Game 32: Williams=Staunton, London 1851

1.e4 e6 2.d4 c5 The earliest recorded example of this defense. **3.d5 exd5 4.exd5 d6 5.c4**

This immediately shores up the pawn at d5, but simultaneously shuts in the White Bf1 **5...Bf5** Black, seeing the d6 pawn is immune to attack, develops the Bc8 to a good square, ensuring smooth queen-side development; incidentally, 6...Bxb1 7.Rxb1 Qa5+ and Qxa2 is threatened. An alternative would have been to wait for White to play Nf3 and reply with ...Bg4, intending Bx(N)f3 **6.Bd3 Bxd3 7.Qxd3 Nf6 8.Nc3 Be7 9.Nf3 O-O 10.O-O Nbd7 11.Qf5 a6 12.Ne2 b5 13.b3**

bxc4 14.bxc4 Rb8 15.Rb1 White, evidently eager to draw, encourages a further piece swap. **15...Rxb1 16.Qxb1 Qb6 17.Qc2** But not 17.Qxb6 Nxb6, when White's c-pawn comes under attack. **17...Rb8 18.Ng3 g6 19.Re1 Bf8 20.Nd2 Qb4** Applying latent pressure against the Re1. **21.a3 Qa5 22.f4 Bg7** The delayed fianchetto. **23.Nf3 Ng4** Intending 24...Bd4+, and if 25.Nxd4?? Qxe1+ **24.Re2 Qc3 25.Ne4** 25.Qxc3 Bxc3 26.Ne4 Rb1! **25...Qa1 26.Re1 Bd4+ 27.Kf1!** 27.Nxd4?? is still bad: 27...Qxd4+ 28.Kh1 Re8! **27...Re8! 28.g3** 28.h3!? f5! 29.hxg4 Rxe4 (29...fxe4 30.Nxd4 Qxd4 31.Bb2+-) 30.gxf5 gxf5=+ **28...f5 29.Nxd6 Re3!** 29...Rxe1+ 30.Nxe1+= **30.Kg2** Fleeing the dangerous back rank; if 30.Rxe3?? Bxe3 wins a piece and the game. **30...Rxe1 31.Nxe1 Ne3+ 32.Bxe3 Qxe1 33.Bxd4** 33.Bf2? Bxf2 34.Qxf2 Qe7 35.N any Qe4+ -+ **33...cxd4 34.c5 Nxc5 35.Qxc5 Qe2+ 36.Kg1 Qe1+ 37.Kg2 Qe2+** Draw. Whew! Whoever said you couldn't learn as much from 'old' games?

Game 33: Krutzfeldt=Stummer, Correspondence 1960

1.d4 c5 2.d5 d6 3.e4 e6 4.c4 exd5 5.exd5 Arriving, via transposition, at the same position as after 1.e4 e6 2.d4 c5 3.d5 exd5 4.exd5 d6 5.c4 **5...Nd7 6.Nc3 Ndf6** Since White has no immediate threats, Black feels justified in spending time on this maneuver, which will avoid queen-side piece congestion. Black's Ng8 will find suitable employment at e7. **7.Nf3 g6 8.Be2 Bg7 9.O-O Ne7**

10.Bf4 a6 Completely preventing Nb5; however, after 10...O-O 11.Nb5 Ne8!, attacking the b2-pawn and threatening to evict the Nb5 with ...a6, seems sufficient. **11.Ng5 O-O 12.Nge4 Ne8**

13.Qd2 f5!? 14.Ng5 Nf6 15.Ne6 Bxe6 16.dxe6 d5 17.cxd5 Nfxd5 18.Nxd5 Nxd5 19.Bc4 Ne7 20.Qd7 b5 21.Be2 Qxd7 22.exd7 Ra7 23.Bd6 Rxd7 24.Bxc5 Bxb2 25.Rad1 Rxd1 26.Rxd1 Re8 27.Bf3 White's two bishops are adequate compensation for the pawn minus; indeed, Black is rapidly forced to give back the material with interest, seeking refuge in a bishops-of-opposite-color ending. **27...Bf6 28.g3 g5 29.Rd6 Kf7 30.Rxa6 g4 31.Be2 Rb8 32.a3 Nd5 33.Bd3 Kg6 34.Rd6 Ne7 35.Rb6 Rxb6 36.Bxb6 Nd5 37.Bc5 Nc3 38.Bb4 Nd5 39.Bxb5 Nxb4 40.axb4 Bc3 41.Be8+ Kg5 42.b5 Bd4 43.Kg2 f4** Draw.

Game 34: Meyer-Hellenschmidt, Correspondence 1969

1.d4 c5 2.d5 e6 3.c4 g6 4.e4 exd5 5.exd5 d6 6.Bd3 Bg7 7.Nc3 Nd7 8.f4 Ne7 9.Nb5? A crude attack on the d6-pawn which Black easily repulses. White was perhaps considering 9...Nf6 10.f5? Nxf5? 11.Bf4, but Black can simply play 10...Bxf5 instead. **9...Nf6 10.Ne2 a6 11.Nbc3 O-O 12.Ng3 b5!**

13.O-O White did not care to enter into the wild complications resulting from 13.cxb5 axb5 14.Bxb5 Nexd5 15.Nxd5 Nxd5 16.Bc6 Nb4!? 17.Bxa8 Re8+ or 13.cxb5 axb5 14.Bxb5 Nexd5 15.Nxd5 Nxd5 16.Qxd5 Qa5+ 17.Bd2 Qxb5 18.Qxa8 Re8+ **13...bxc4 14.Bxc4 Nf5 15.Nce2 Re8 16.Nxf5 Bxf5 17.Ng3 Ng4!** Exploiting White's critical dark-square weaknesses. **18.Nxf5 gxf5 19.Qc2 Bd4+ 20.Kh1**

(See the diagram at the top of the next page)

20...Nxh2! Splat! White Resigns.

Game 35: Fedorowicz=Murey, New York 1983

1.d4 e6 2.e4 c5 3.d5 exd5 4.exd5 d6 5.c4 Ne7 6.Nc3 g6 7.Ne4

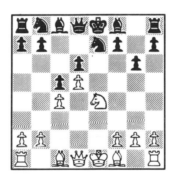

Caveman chess, threatening Nf6mate, but there's more to it than that... **7...Bg7 8.Qa4+ Kf8** Since the Ne4 is hitting d6, Black cannot block the check. **9.Nf3 Bf5 10.Bd3 Nd7 11.Qc2 Bxe4 12.Bxe4 b5 13.cxb5 Qa5+ 14.Nd2** Or 14.Bd2 Qxb5 15.Bc3 **14...Qxb5 15.Bd3 Qb7 16.O-O Be5** If 16...Qxe4?? 17.Be4; 16...Nxe4? 17.Be4 **17.Nc4 Kg7 18.Be4 Rhd8 19.Nxe5 Nxe5 20.f4 Nd7 21.b3 Ng8 22.Bb2+ Ngf6 23.g4 Kg8 24.Bf3 h6 25.h4 Qb4 26.g5 Nh7 27.Bg2 Rab8 28.Bc3 Qb6 29.Kh2 c4 30.b4 hxg5 31.hxg5 Re8 32.Rae1 Re3 33.Rxe3 Qxe3 34.Rf3 Qe7 35.Qf2 Re8** Who's trapping whom? For the loss of the exchange White gets two connected queen-side passers. **36.Qxa7 Ne5 37.Qd4 Nxf3+ 38.Bxf3 f6 39.Bg4 Ra8 40.Be6+ Kf8 41.b5 Qa7 42.b6 Qxa2+ 43.Kg3 Qb3 44.b7 Qxb7 45.Qxc4 Qa6** Draw.

2B: White plays 5.g3

Smirnov/Konstantinopolsky, Moscow 1966 saw: 1.d4 c5 2.d5 e6 3.e4 exd5 4.exd5 d6 5.g3 Nf6 6.Bg2 Be7 7.a4 O-O 8.Na3 b6 9.Ne2 Na6 10.Nc4 Nc7 11.O-O Re8 12.h3 Bf8 13.Re1 Bf5 and Black had a comfortable game. With a White pawn on d5, the fianchetto development Bf1-g2 is not particularly dangerous to Black.

**Chapter 3: 1.e4 e6 2.d4 c5 3.d5 exd5 4.exd5 d6
5.Nf3 Bg4**

In this variation, White does not care to employ the
'exact' move order 5.Nc3 > 6.Be2 / 7.Nf3, undisturbed by
Barcza's plan of 5...Bg4 > 6...Bx(N)f3.

Game 36: Filip-Barcza, Sofia 1957

1.d4 c5 2.d5 e6 3.Nc3 Nf6 4.e4 d6 5.Nf3 exd5 6.exd5
White cannot get any advantage after 6.Nxd5, since Black is
not compelled to play into 6...Nxd5 7.Qxd5 Nc6 (hoping to
'embarrass' the White queen with ...Be6) 8.Ng5 Qc7 9.Bc4
Ne5 10.Bb5+ Bd7 (10...Nc6? loses to 11.Nxf7 Qxf7 12.Bxc6+)
11.a4, where White is better, but instead can reply 6...Be6!,
obtaining rough equality after 7.Bg5 Bxd5 8.exd5 Be7 **6...Bg4**

Many sources, including ECO, give an incorrect move
order for the beginning of this game, apparently to make it 'fit'
into various opening classifications. Magyar Sakkelet (which
contains Barcza's original annotations), Deutsche Schachzeitung, and The British Chess Magazine all agree on the move
order presented here. **7.Be2 Bxf3** Black exchanges bishop for
knight before White can play Nf3-d2-c4, even though this
'costs' a tempo, since it occurs unprovoked by h2-h3. **8.Bxf3
Be7 9.O-O O-O 10.Bf4 Nbd7** It may seem surprising, but
Black possesses what chances may exist: he has prospects of

57

advancing his queen-side pawns, his d6-pawn is adequately defended, and White's bishops lack scope, particularly the light-squared Bf3, which is limited by its own d5-pawn. **11.Re1 Ne8** Black effects a 'changing of the guard' on his d6-pawn, freeing his Be7 **12.Be2 a6** A move with two purposes. The first, and most obvious, is to expand with ...b5. The second, restraint of the Be2, shows a positional understanding of the 'threat' created by White's last move. White would very much like to play Bb5, followed by exchanging his 'bad' bishop for one of Black's knights. The road to hell, however, is paved with good intentions; although White feels forced to stop ...b5, his exchanging plan costs time and permits Black to implement one of his own. **13.a4** Stopping any thoughts of an immediate ...b5, but White could have prevented Black's upcoming plan with 13.Qd2, which would have been better on move 12, as well. If 13.Qd2 b5 14.a4 b4 15.Ne4 Ndf6 16.Ng3 Nc7 17.Bc4, things are approximately equal. **13...Bg5**

A pure positional concept borrowed from analogous situations in the Czech Benoni. Even though the symmetrical Barcza-Larsen pawn structures differ from their true Benoni counterparts (no rival pawn majorities), and would seem to invalidate comparison of the systems, some Benoni themes are equally relevant to the Barcza-Larsen. Here, Black's dark-squared bishop, at least during the opening and early middle-game, is very much a 'bad' bishop, and so Barcza seeks to exchange it off. His persistence in this regard is part of what makes this game so striking. **14.Bg3 Bf6 15.Bf1 Be5** Consistent but probably inaccurate, as White has hesitated in playing a4-a5, cramping the queen-side. 16...b6 was therefore better, because White cannot prevent ...Be5 without incurring some positional weakening. **16.Bxe5** White can no longer avoid the exchange, since 16.f4? weakens the king-side and is easily answered by 16...Bd4+, when 17.Bf2 is probably best anyway. **16...Nxe5 17.a5** Fixing Black's queen-side pawns and preventing Black from playing ...b6, with the idea of ...Nc7,...Rb8, and ...b5. It's ironic that such a well-motivated move contributes to White's undoing in the endgame. **17...Nf6 18.Qd2 Qc7** Black clears the back rank so that he can exchange his rooks off along the open e-file and head for a good knight vs. bad bishop ending. **19.Na4 Rae8 20.Nb6** A nice outpost, but Black is easily able to exchange knights. **20...Qd8** Some caution, however, must be exercised: if 20...Nfd7? 21.f4! Nxb6?? 22.axb6! wins a piece. **21.h3** White was worried about 21.f4 Neg4 22.h3 Nh6 23.g4 Ne4 24.Qd3 f5 25.gxf5 Nf6, where Black is better, since he can easily regain the pawn, and more. Nonetheless, 21.f4 was the right move, because after 21...Neg4 22.h3 Nh6 White can instead play 23.Bd3, controlling e4. So, after 21.f4, Black would reply 21...Ned7, and White could get his knight to a good square with 22.Nc4. **21...Nfd7** The right knight, so as to keep c4 covered. **22.Nxd7** And now it's too late for 22.f4?, since after 22...Nxb6 23.fxe5 Nd7 Black grips the e5-square; 24.exd6 Ne5. **22...Nxd7 23.Rxe8 Rxe8 24.Re1 Nf6?!** A direct approach, but time-trouble caused Black to miss a stronger plan: 24...g6 > ...Kg7/...Qf6, was better per Barcza. **25.Bd3** Even so, White is beginning to feel uncomfortable. The far-flung pawn on a5 is being observed greedily by the Black queen and Black also threatens ...Rxe1 and ...Nxd5. White's move defends the d5-pawn tactically: 25...Nxd5? 26.Rxe8+ Qxe8 27.Bxh7+ Kxh7 28.Qxd5; if 25...Rxe1+? 26.Qxe1 Nxd5 27.Qe4 Nf6 28.Qxb7 leaves White with the better game. **25...g6** Renewing the threat of ...Rxe1+ and ...Nxd5. **26.c4** White's bad bishop is getting worse. **26...Nd7 27.Rxe8+ Qxe8 28.Qc3 Qe5?** The question mark may seem a bit harsh, since Black surely wants to exploit White's bishop with queens off the board, but it is Barcza's own annotation. The reason: at the moment, Black's queen is a stronger piece than White's, so 28...Ne5, and a little patience, was called for. **29.Qxe5** If White does not trade, Black's queen is left in a dominating position; e.g., 28.Qc2? Qe1+ > 29...Qxa5; 28.Qd2 Qd4 > 29...Ne5 **29...Nxe5 30.Be2 Kf8** Black has his desired endgame, but with best play, White can probably draw. **31.f4 Nd7 32.Bd1** Hoping for 32...Ke8 33.Ba4 **32...Ke7 33.Ba4** This certainly seems logical. Black didn't walk into the pin, but the threat of taking the knight is still serious. Or is it? **33...b6!?**

A magnificent swindling attempt. **34.Bxd7 Kxd7 35.axb6??** The fatal error! White can draw with 35.g4 bxa5 36.Kf2 a4 37.Ke3 Kc7 38.Kd3 Kb6 39.Kc2! (and only thus, so as to answer ...Ka5 with Kc3, seizing the opposition) 39...Ka5 40.Kc3 h5 (or 40...a3 41.bxa3 Ka4 42.Kb2) 41.gxh5 gxh5 42.f5! h4 43.f6 **35...Kc8 36.Kf2 Kb7 37.Ke3 Kxb6 38.Kd3 Ka5 39.Kc3 Ka4 40.g3** 40.b3+ Ka3; White's king-side pawns become fixed and Black will win the b-pawn. 40.b4 was the last desperate try, with the probable sequel: 40...cxb4+ 41.Kb2 Ka5! (There is still room for error, e.g., 41...a5? 42.c5 Kb5 43.c6, with a draw; even worse is 41...b3?? 42.c5 Kb5 43.c6 and White actually wins.) 42.Kb3 Kb6 43.Kxb4 a5+ 44.Ka4 Kc5 winning. **40...f5 41.g4 h5** At this point, the game was adjourned. White sealed 42.gxh5, but, realizing further resistance was futile... **White Resigned.** After 42...gxh5 43.h4 a5 44.b3+ Ka3 45.Kc2 a4 46.bxa4 Kxa4 47.Kc3 Ka3, Black gains the opposition, and with it, the game.

Game 37: Karpov+Pronin, Moscow Univ. Champ., 1968-69

1.e4 e6 2.d4 c5 3.d5 exd5 4.exd5 d6 5.Nf3 Bg4 6.Be2 a6?! Inconsistent with Black's strategy, since White can now play Nf3-d2, avoiding Bx(N)f3. It is interesting that Karpov allows this anyway. **7.a4** 7.O-O!? b5 8.a4 += is given by

Karpov. Black's queen-side expansion is less appropriate when White has not already committed himself to Nc3, because [after 7.a4 b4] White may strike at the Black pawn with c2-c3. **7...Bxf3** Since White permits it, why not? Karpov's notes, however, give 7...Nf6 8.O-O Be7 9.Nc3 O-O 10.Nd2! +-. The difficult thing to understand is, if Karpov recognized the value of preserving his knight and trading light-squared bishops, why pass up three opportunities to do so from move 7 through move 9? **8.Bxf3 Be7 9.O-O Nd7 10.Nd2** Since the pawn on d5 is adequately defended, White takes the opportunity to be flexible in placing his queen's knight; now Nc4 is possible. This theme recurs in Gligoric+ Barcza, Game 38. **10...b6?** Karpov gives 10...Ngf6!? and that move is surely more natural. As Filip-Barcza showed, a5 by White is not always a problem. **11.Re1** A better move would be 11.Nc4! > 12.Bf4 and 13.Re1; if 11...b5, then 12.axb5 axb5 13.Rxa8 Qxa8 14.Na3 Qb7 15.c4 +-. **11...Ne5**

If 11...Ngf6, 12.Nc4 O-O 13.Bf4 hammers at the weak d6-pawn and forces Black to play 13...Ne8 (13...Nb8? 14.Rxe7! Qxe7 15.Bxd6), after which White will mass his heavy pieces along the open e-file. **12.Rxe5!** An alert combination. White exploits the latent threats on the h1-a8 diagonal. **12...dxe5 13.d6 Bxd6 14.Bc6+ Kf8?!** Even after the slightly better 14...Ke7 15.Bxa8 Qxa8 16.Nc4 Qb8 17.Bg5+, White would have excellent compensation. **15.Bxa8 Qxa8 16.Nc4 Bc7 17.Be3! Ne7** 17...a5 18.Qd7 Qd8 19.Rd1 +-. **18.a5 bxa5** If 18...b5 instead, then 19.Nb6 Qc6 20.Bxc5! f6 21.Qd5 Qxd5 22.Nxd5 Bd8 23.Nb4 and White is clearly winning. **19.Bxc5 Qc6** 19...Qd8 runs into 20.Nxe5! (>21.Nc6) 20...Qxd1+ 21.Rxd1, and if 21...Bxe5?? 22.Rd8mate. **20.Nxe5! Qe8**

20...Bxe5 21.Qd8+ and mates. **21.Qd4 h5 22.Re1** Black Resigns. One look at the hideous final position of Black's pieces is enough to tell you he completely misplayed the opening. Of course, the fact he was facing a future world champion had something to do with that. A little-known game by Karpov that demonstrates his considerable combinative talent.

Game 38: Gligoric+Barcza, Ljubljana 1969

1.d4 e6 2.e4 c5 3.d5 exd5 4.exd5 d6 5.Nf3 Bg4 6.Be2 Bxf3 7.Bxf3 Be7 8.O-O Nf6 9.Na3! As mentioned in Karpov-Pronin, with the d5-pawn securely defended, White can afford to take time to make sure this piece reaches the best square. **9...O-O 10.Nc4 Nbd7** Again, the absence of a knight on c3 makes ...b5 susceptible to a later a4; e.g., 10...b5 11.Ne3 > 12.a4 **11.a4** White could have prevented Black's rather surprising next move with 11.Re1. **11...Ne5!**

An unexpected twist from Barcza, which looks bad at first blush: why give White a passed pawn? The reason is that Black will successfully blockade the passer by maneuvering his remaining knight to d6, in front of the pawn. As Nimzowitsch noted in his first published work, Die Blockade (The Blockade), in 1925, such a blockading piece stands well because: 1. Enemy frontal attack is impossible. 2. The blockading square is often made accessible to the rooks, which later assault the passed pawn (although in this case, White has the potential supporting move c2-c4). 3. The blockading piece retains enough elasticity to quickly move to another area as needed.

Nimzowitsch also noted that a successful blockade is more than just an isolated, local measure against a passed pawn - he believed that the blockade caused other enemy pieces to suffer, as well. In the present situation, restraint of the d5-pawn does cause the light-squared Bf3 to diminish somewhat in scope. Conversely, Black's 'bad' bishop will become a bit stronger, since it will have access to the a1-h8 diagonal via f6. **12.Nxe5 dxe5 13.Re1** White gets no more than equality from 13.d6 Bxd6 14.Bxb7 Rb8. **13...Qd6** First things first, since the e5-pawn was threatened. **14.Qd3 Ne8 15.Qe4 Bf6 16.Be3 Qc7 17.Qc4 b6 18.Qg4 Nd6** Black's mission is accomplished. **19.Be2 g6** Strengthening the squares around the king (against Be2-d3, attacking h7), since the best defender, the knight, is no longer on f6. Black's bishop will control the weakened dark squares and a post for the knight is incidentally created on f5. **20.Bb5 Nf5 21.c3** Keeping the knight out of d4. **21...Rad8 22.Rad1 Bg7** Gligoric recommended 22...Nxe3, hoping to hold the draw by virtue of the opposite-colored bishops and further blockade with ...Rd6, but the knight is so flexible it seems a shame to swap it off. **23.Bg5 f6 24.Bc1 Nd6 25.Qh4!** >Re1-e3-h3 **25...Rf7 26.f4 Nxb5!?** Black chooses to part with his knight in order to compromise White's queen-side pawns; 26...e4 is countered by 27.f5! **27.axb5 c4 28.fxe5 fxe5 29.d6 Rxd6 30.Rxd6 Qxd6 31.Qxc4 Qc7 32.Qd5 Qd7** Black is eager to exchange queens, and White has little option but to acquiesce. **33.Rd1 Qxd5 34.Rxd5 Rc7 35.Be3 Kf8 36.Kf2 Ke7 37.Ke2 Ke6** Allowing White to penetrate to the back rank, but Black can defend easily. **38.Rd8 Bf6 39.Rd1 Be7 40.Ra1** Attacking Black's only real weakness. **40...Kd5 41.Ra4 Bc5 42.Bd2 Bd6?** After 42...Rf7, Black can count on a successful defense: 43.Kd3 Rf2 44.b4?? e4+ 45.Kc2 Be3; 43.Kd3 Rf2 44.Rxa7?? e4+ 45.Kc2 Be3; 43.Kd3 Rf2 44.c4+ Ke6 45.Rxa7? e4+ 46.Kc3 e3 47.Be1 Rf1 48.b4 Bxb4+ 49.Kxb4 Rxe1; 43.Kd3 Rf2 44.c4+ Ke6 45.b4! Be7? 46.Rxa7 Rxg2 47.Ra6 +-; 45...e4+! 46.Kxe4 Rxd2 47.bxc5 bxc5 48.Ra6+ Rd6 49.Rxa7 Rd4+ draws. **43.Kd3 Rf7 44.c4+ Ke6 45.Be3 Kf5? 46.g4+ Ke6** 46...Kxg4?? 47.c5+. **47.Ra6! Rc7 48.b3** White has forced Black's pieces into uncomfortably defensive roles by mobilizing his queen-side pawn majority; c5 will become a continual threat. **48...e4+** Black now exchanges off his isolated pawn to obtain a king-side pawn majority, but White's pawn advance on the opposite wing is just too fast.

49.Kxe4 Bxh2 50.c5 Re7

Setting one last trap. **51.g5!** Avoiding 51.cxb6? Kf7+
52.Kf3 axb6 53.Rxb6?? Rxe3+! and Black wins. **51...Kd7+
52.Kd3 Bb8 53.b4!** An echo of the previous trap is heard:
53.cxb6? axb6 54.Rxb6?? Rxe3+! **53...Kc8 54.Ra1 Rd7+
55.Kc4 Re7 56.Bd4 Re4 57.Kd3 Rg4 58.Rh1 bxc5 59.bxc5
Rxg5** Trying to impede White by 59...Rg3+ is met by 60.Kc4
Rg4 61.Re1. **60.Rxh7 Rd5 61.Kc4 Rd7 62.Rh6 g5** Forced, but
now White's rook is able to actively assist the pawns' advance.
**63.Bf6 >64.Rh8+. 63...Bf4 64.Rh8+ Kc7 65.Ra8 Kb7
66.c6+ Kxa8 67.cxd7 Bc7 68.Bxg5 a6** Gligoric's winning
technique has been finely calculated, since he had to consider
Black's drawing threat: sacrificing the bishop for one pawn
while attempting to trade the other set of pawns. If 68...Kb7,
White wins with 69.d8(Q) Bxd8 70.Bxd8 a6 71.b6. **69.bxa6
Ka7 70.Kb5 Bb6** Ending the agony. **71.Be3** Black Resigns.

**Chapter 4: 1.e4 e6 2.d4 c5 3.d5 exd5 4.exd5 exd5
5.Nf3 or 5.Nc3: Black plays ...g6**

Game 39: Uhlmann+Kunze, East German Championship, 1954

1.d4 c5 2.d5 e6 3.e4 exd5 4.exd5 d6 5.Nf3 g6? 6.Bg5!
Trouble comes from an unexpected source; instead of immediately pressuring the d6-pawn, anticipating its being weakened by ...Bf8-g7, White first forces Black to make an unpleasant move. If 6...Ne7, White has the disruptive check 7.Bb5+ followed by 8.Qe2, making it difficult for Black to castle. **6...f6 7.Bf4 Bg7 8.Nc3 a6** Nc3-b5 was already a threat. **9.Ne4** But so was this. **9...Bf8** Black's pieces, after nine moves, are still in their starting blocks. **10.Qe2 Kf7 11.h4 Bf5 12.h5 g5**

At this point, Uhlmann could have crashed through with 13.N(either)xg5+ fxg5 14.Nxg5+, because after 14...Kf6 15.Ne6 Qc8 (And not 15...Bxe6?? because of 16.Qxe6+ Kg7 17.h6+ Nxh6 18.Bxh6 mate) 16.Bg5+ Kf7 17.Qf3 regaining the piece with two pawns interest, or 14...Kg7 15.h6+ Nxh6 16.Ne6+ Bxe6 17.Bxh6+ Kg6 18.Qxe6+ Qf6 19.Bd3 mate, Black is washed up. Instead, Uhlmann chose 13.Bxg5, allowing Black to defend. A few additional moves in the actual game continuation are given. **13.Bxg5 Qe7 14.Ng3 Qxe2+ 15.Bxe2 Bxc2 16.Bf4 Nd7 17.b3 Re8 18.Nh4 Bd3 19.Nhf5 Bxe2 20.Nxe2 Ne5** And Black ultimately lost after White exploited the weakened king-side.

Game 40: Muller-Stummer, Correspondence 1960-61

1.e4 e6 2.d4 c5 3.d5 exd5 4.exd5 d6 5.Nc3 a6 Black realizes that many of his troubles resulting from ...g6 are linked to Bb5+ and/or Nb5, so he prevents such moves. **6.a4** White is naturally reluctant to allow ...b5, but one suspects that this might not be such a problem, since the Nc3, if evicted by ...b7-b5-b4, would happily swing over to e4, attacking the d6-pawn. Consequently, 6.Bf4 deserved consideration. **6...Nd7** The same idea as in Krutzfeldt=Stummer, Game 33, where White had played c4. Black intends to play ...g6,...Ndf6, ...Bg7, and ...Ne7. **7.Nf3 g6 8.Bf4** 8.Bg5!? **8...Ndf6 9.Bc4 Bg7 10.O-O Ne7 11.Qd2 O-O?!** Black had a more forceful plan available here: 11...h6 > 12.Re1 g5!, followed by ...O-O and an eventual ...Ng6, achieving an ideal posting for his pieces. White's only real attempt to counter this idea would involve a risky sacrifice on g5. **12.Bh6 Re8 13.Bxg7 Kxg7 14.Rfe1 Bd7 15.Qf4 Qc7 16.Ng5 Bf5 17.Nce4 Bxe4** Even in lines where Black fianchettos, seeking a good knight vs. bad bishop ending remains a valid plan. **18.Nxe4 Nxe4 19.Rxe4 b5 20.Ba2 c4 21.Qd2 Ng8 22.Rae1 Rxe4 23.Rxe4 Nf6 24.Qc3 g5!? 25.h4 Kg6 26.h5+ Nxh5 27.Qd2 Nf6 28.Rd4 Qe7 29.c3 h6 30.b3 cxb3 31.Bxb3 Re8 32.axb5 axb5 33.Kf1 Qe5 34.g3 Kg7 35.Bc2 Qe7 36.Rb4 Qd7 37.Bd1**

37...Nxd5! 38.Bg4 38.Qxd5? Qh3+ 39.Qg2 Re1+! **38...Qc6 39.Qd4+ Nf6 40.f3 Re5** White Resigns.

This seems like a good place to draw some preliminary conclusions about the ...g6 line and present additional analysis. When Black is intent on fianchettoing after 1.e4 e6 2.d4 c5

3.d5 exd5 4.exd5 d6, it appears that some preparation is needed first, since an immediate ...g6 can become susceptible to Bf4 or Bg5, attacking the weakened dark squares. Muller-Stummer suggested that after 5.Nc3, 5...a6 might be the move, avoiding the piece congestion following a possible Bb5+ by White and countering dark-square problems after ...g6 by shuttling the Nb8 to f6.

Stummer's ...Nb8-d7-f6 perhaps inspired the theorist Gunderam to develop an alternative plan, involving the establishment of a 'concrete'-like strong-point position based on the unusual move ...f6.

Gunderam's idea is first considered after 1.e4 e6 2.d4 c5 3.d5 exd5 4.exd5 d6 5.Nf3: Black plays 5...Nbd7. Black's apparent passivity is then best tested by 6.c4, anchoring the d5-pawn, since Black has given up the ...Bc8-g4x(N)f3 idea. Black therefore continues with 6...g6, and answers the bothersome 7.Bg5 with 7...f6! The continuation is then likely to follow 8.Bh4 Bg7 9.Nc3 a6 (Preventing 10.Nb5) 10.Bd3 Nge7 11.O-O O-O (Diagram) and Black prepares to cast his queen's knight in concrete with ...Ne5.

It's useful to look at lines where White plays c4 even earlier, since transposition may occur from 1.d4. For example, after 1.d4 e6 2.c4 c5 3.d5 d6 4.e4 exd5 5.exd5, Black again plays the key move 5...Nbd7, when 6.Nc3 g6 7.Bf4 can be met by 7...f6, the 'left support post' for a prospective ...Ne5. Now, 8.Nb5 is answered by 8...Ne5, so White probably does best to develop calmly: 8.Nf3 Ne5 9.h3 Bg7 10.Be2 Nh6 11.Qd2 Nf7 12.O-O (If 12.O-O-O, Black organizes play on the queen-side with 12...a6 13.Re1 Bd7 and ...b5) 12...O-O 13.Rfe1, and now, one of Black's tactical ideas is revealed with 13...g5.

(See the diagram at the top of the next page)

Whether White opts for 14.Bg3 Bf5 or 14.Bh2 Bf5 15.g4 Bg6, Black has a reasonable position.

Should White decide to do without h3 and play 1.d4 c5 2.d5 e6 3.e4 exd5 4.exd5 d6 5.c4 Nbd7 6.Nc3 g6 7.Bf4 f6 8.Nf3 Ne5 9.Be2, the same recipe of 9...Nh6 10.Qd2 Nf7

11.O-O Bg7 12.Rfe1 O-O is satisfactory.

The maneuver Bf1-d3 seems less appropriate for White in this line, since the Nf3 is given less support and the Bd3 may itself become a target: 1.d4 c5 2.d5 e6 3.e4 exd5 4.exd5 d6 5.c4 Nbd7 6.Nc3 g6 7.Bf4 f6 8.Nf3 Ne5 9.h3 Bg7 10.Bd3 Nh6 11.O-O (11.Qd2?! is obviously bad; 11...Nxf3+ 12.gxf3 Nf7 intending ...Ne5 just leaves White in a bad way.) 11...O-O (White must now deal with Black's threat to activate his pieces with ...Nxd3 and ...Bf5/...g5.) 12.Nxe5 fxe5!, with ...Bf5 to follow.

Another important variation occurs when White plays Nc3 instead of c4. This is most frequently encountered after 1.e4 e6 2.d4 c5 3.d5 exd5 4.exd5 d6 5.Nc3, as in Muller-Stummer above. Since White has not ruled out Bb5+ by playing the blocking move c4, Black is probably justified in continuing with 5...a6. 6.a4 seems the most logical reply, and now Black plays the key-move 6...Nbd7. After 7.Bf4 f6 8.Nf3 (Better than 8.Bd3 g6 9.Qe2+ Ne5 10.Bg3 Ne7) 8...g6 9.Be2 Nh6 (This first - before White prevents it by Qd2) 10.Qd2 Nf7 11.O-O Bg7 12.Rfe1 Nde5 13.h3 O-O and Black is ready to expand outward from his 'concrete' bastion on the king-side with ...g5 and ...Bf5.

Again, White can do without h3; e.g., after the first 12 moves as above, 13.Rab1 (intending b4) is an option. Then, 13...O-O 14.b4 b6 15.bxc5 bxc5 leaves White wondering how to get at the Black position. 16.Nh4?! appears to be too provocative: 16...g5! 17.Bxe5 Nxe5 18.Nf3 (18.f4 appears more to the point, since after 18...gxh4 19.fxe5 fxe5 White has some initiative for his pawn.) 18...Ng6! (Black suddenly threatens to win a piece with 19...g4!) 19.Qc1 (White is loathe to weaken his king-side with 19.h3, but this move allows Black's attack to roll on unchecked.) 19...g4 20.Nd2 f5 21.Rb3 Qh4 22.Nc4 Bd4 23.Nd1 f4 24.Qa3 Bf5 25.c3? g3! White Resigns, as in Game 41: Emanon-Fields, Tampa 1990.

Should White exchange off the Black knight when it comes to e5, Black obtains a good position with ...fxe5, e.g., after the first 12 moves as above, 13.Nxe5 fxe5. Now the Bf4 must make a decision; 14.Bg3 allows 14...Bh6!, but after 14.Be3, Black can continue his dark-square play with 14...Qh4.

All well and good, but since Gunderam's pioneering analyses from 1957-1961, more aggressive methods have been developed for attacking Black's fianchettoed positions. One such method is the berserk attack based on an early h2-h4: 1.e4 e6 2.d4 c5 3.d5 exd5 4.exd5 d6 5.Nc3 a6 6.a4 Nd7 7.Nf3 g6 8.h4!? How should Black continue? 8...h5 seems the most reliable, although White can try to exploit the weakened dark squares with 9.Bg5. Black may then be able to erect a defense with 9...Be7 and 10...Ndf6, intending ...Bf5 or ...Bg4. An alternative plan for Black involves the ugly but thematic early ...f6, e.g., 1.e4 e6 2.d4 c5 3.d5 exd5 4.exd5 d6 5.Nc3 a6 6.a4 Nd7 7.Nf3 f6, deferring ...g6 until White has possibly castled kingside. If White insists on making Black show his hand with 8.Bf4, Black can consider an immediate 8...Ne5!? or play 8...g6 anyway; if White charges forth with 9.h4, Black may reply 9...Nh6 10.h5 g5!, refusing to let White open the h-file.

Finally, we should examine an attempt by White to disrupt Black's intended ...Ng8-h6-f7 maneuver with an early Bf4 and Qd2. After 1.e4 e6 2.d4 c5 3.d5 exd5 4.exd5 d6 5.Nc3 a6 6.a4 Nd7 7.Bf4 g6 8.Qd2, Black may shift gears and try Stummer's set-up with 8...Ndf6 9.Nf3 Bg7 10.Bc4 Ne7, and after 11.O-O, opt for the 11...h6 12.Re1 g5 with ...O-O and ...Ng6 plan.

Game 42: Jamieson+Levy, Bath 1963

1.e4 e6 2.d4 c5 3.d5 exd5 4.exd5 d6 5.Nf3 Nf6 6.Nc3 g6 Black naturally wants to give his pieces the widest possible scope, and fianchettoing the bishop certainly looks more active than positioning it at e7. But there is a big drawback: the pawn at d6 is denied the bishop's protection, and Black must often resort to the retreat Nf6-e8 after White has played a bishop to f4 and/or a knight to c4.   **7.Bb5+** This disruptive check makes it impossible for Black to castle and fianchetto. **7...Bd7 8.O-O Bg7** Black chooses to fianchetto, since blocking the upcoming check along the e-file with ...Be7 would allow White to play Bh6. **9.Re1+ Kf8 10.Bf4 Ne8 11.Qe2** Setting a diabolical trap. **11...a6**

Into which Black promptly falls. **12.Qxe8+!! Bxe8 13.Bxd6+** The point! **13...Kg8** And not 13...Qxd6 14.Rxe8 mate! **14.Rxe8+ Qxe8 15.Bxe8 Bf6** and Black Resigns. A drastic lesson in the difficulties incurred in the ...g6 line.

Here is another miniature demonstrating a quick bash of ...g6:

Game 43: Meystre+Klein, Correspondence 1968

1.e4 e6 2.d4 c5 3.d5 exd5 4.exd5 d6 5.Nf3 Nd7 Emulating Stummer (See Games 33 and 40), but Black's follow-up indicates he has not completely absorbed the nuances of this approach. **6.Bf4 g6 7.Nbd2** Is there any doubt where this piece is going? **7...Ngf6 8.Nc4 Nb6 9.Qe2+ Kd7**

Since 9...Be7 fails to 10.Nxd6+, Black didn't have to waste much time making this move. White's next, however, results in a considerable saving of postage. **10.Nfe5+!** Black Resigns.

Game 44: Maksimovic-Hulak, Nis 1985

1.d4 e6 2.e4 c5 3.d5 exd5 4.exd5 d6 5.Nc3 Nf6 6.Be2 g6 If White opts for the 'exact' move order with 6.Be2 to deter ...Bc8-g4x(N)f3, then Black may well be justified in playing ...g6, since White does not have a disruptive check along the e-file, and Bb5+ will cost an additional tempo. **7.Nf3 Bg7 8.O-O O-O 9.Bf4** White takes direct aim at the weak d6-pawn. **9...Bg4** Black would like to play 10...Bxf3 to prevent the knight from reaching c4. **10.Nd2** White naturally refuses to cooperate. **10...Bxe2 11.Qxe2 Nh5**

Black forces the Bf4 from the h2-b8 diagonal; 12.Bg3 would be answered by 12...Nxg3, so White is left with little choice. **12.Be3 f5** A crude tactical threat (13...f4) that has positional merit: Black takes the e4-square away from White's knights. **13.Nc4 a6 14.a4 Re8** Again threatening ...f4. Black is starting to push White around too much for the first player's liking, and after this move, Maksimovic feels compelled to start a tactical melee. **15.Bg5?! Rxe2 16.Bxd8 Bxc3** Black is willing to part with his good bishop to fracture and devalue White's pawns. **17.bxc3 Nd7 18.Bg5 Ndf6 19.Rab1** If 19.Nxd6, then 19...Nxd5. **19...Ne4 20.Bh6 b5 21.axb5 Nxc3** A handy little zwischenzug that virtually forces White to part with the exchange, since ...Nxb5, winning a pawn, is threatened. **22.b6 Nxb1 23.Rxb1 Nf6 24.Kf1 Ree8** The c2-pawn is meaningless; Black regroups to halt and win the passed b-pawn. **25.Nxd6 Reb8 26.c4 a5** Showing who's in charge here. White cannot cope with Black's threats to queen his a-pawn and win White's b-pawn. **27.Bf4 Nd7 28.b7 Ra7 29.Ra1 Ra6 30.h4 a4 31.Ra3 h6 32.Rg3 Nf8 33.Nxf5 Rxb7 34.Nxh6+ Kh7 35.Ra3 Rb3** White Resigns.

Game 45: Fields+Moore, Cincinnati 1985

1.d4 Nf6 2.Nc3 c5 3.d5 e6 4.e4 exd5 5.exd5 d6 And we reach the Barcza-Larsen via a transposition from the Veresov System. **6.Nf3 g6 7.Be2** 7.Bb5+ is a strong alternative. **7...Bg7 8.O-O O-O 9.Nd2 Na6 10.Nc4 Nc7 11.a4** Restraining any queen-side counterplay with ...b5. **11...b6** Preventing a4-a5. **12.Bf4 Nfe8!?** 12...Nce8, maintaining control over e4, was a solid but passive alternative; the text is much sharper. **13.Re1** White passed on the natural 13.Ne4, since Black could defend with 13...Bb7! 14.Nexd6 Bxd5 15.Nxe8 Nxe8; however, the eccentric 13...Be5?! gives White a good game after 14.Nxe5 dxe5 15.Bh6! (If 15.Bxe5? Qxd5) 15...Ng7 16.c4. **13...Rb8?**

Black underestimates the danger. 13...Bb7, pressuring the d5-pawn, was much better. White must then decide if ...Bxc3, winning the d5-pawn, is a serious threat; taking the time to defend the pawn with 14.Bf3 means White must reckon with the speculative 14...g5!? (intending 15...f5) or 14...Ba6. Therefore, 14.Qd2 calls Black's bluff, but after 14...Bxc3! 15.bxc3 Bxd5 (15...Nxd5? 16.Bh6 Ng7 17.Bf3!) 16.Bh6 Ng7 17.Ne3 Bc6 18.Red1 it is doubtful if White has compensation for the sacrificed pawn. **14.Ne4!** Now this thematic move is strengthened by the latent threat to the Rb8. **14...f5** One move too late. If 14...Bb7, White can safely play 15.Nexd6: 15...Nxd5 (15...Bxd5 16.Nxe8!) 16.Nxb7 Rxb7 17.Bf3 Rd7 (17...Bd4 18.Bh6) 18.Ne5! **15.Nexd6 Nxd6 16.Bxd6 Re8** 16...Bxb2? 17.Bxc7. **17.c3 Ba6 18.Bg3** Maintaining the unpleasant pin on the Nc7. **18...Ra8 19.Ne3 Bxe2 20.Rxe2 Bh6   >** 21...f4 **21.Bxc7 Qxc7 22.Nc4 Bf8 23.Qe1 Kf7 24.Rd1 Rad8 25.Ne5+ Kg7 26.Nc6 Rxe2 27.Qxe2 Rd6 28.c4 a6 29.Re1 Kg8 30.Qe8 b5 31.Re7!** Black resigns.

Chapter 5: 1.e4 e6 2.d4 c5 3.d5 exd5 4.exd5 d6: White plays Bb5+

Game 46: Prokopp=Stummer, Correspondence 1960

1.e4 e6 2.d4 c5 3.Nf3 b6

Avoiding transposition to the Sicilian; also see Game 5: Bergsma-Diemer. **4.Nc3 d6 5.Bb5+ Bd7 6.O-O a6 7.Bxd7+ Nxd7 8.Be3 Ngf6 9.h3** This is probably unnecessary, since with the immediate 9.Nd2 White can continue as in the game and simultaneously prevent ...Ng4. **9...Qc7 10.Nd2 Be7 11.Qf3** 11.a4 is satisfactory and 11.f4 would be more aggressive; g3, however, would be weak as a result of 9.h3. **11...O-O 12.d5 exd5 13.exd5** And, after a rather lengthy transposition, we arrive at a standard Bb5+ position where the light-squared bishops have been exchanged. Black is doing fine, though, because his queen-side pawn initiative is now unchecked. **13...b5! 14.Nde4 Nxe4 15.Nxe4 Nf6 16.Ng3 Nd7 17.Nf5 Bf6 18.c3 Ne5 19.Qg3 Kh8 20.Bf4 Qd7 21.Ne3 Rfe8 22.Rad1 Rad8 23.Bxe5 dxe5 24.Rfe1 g6** Draw. More proof that Black can avoid being dragged, kicking and screaming, into the Sicilian.

Game 47: O'Kelly-Larsen, Palma de Mallorca 1967

1.d4 e6 2.e4 c5 3.d5 exd5 4.exd5 d6 5.Nf3 Nf6 6.Nc3 Be7 7.Bb5+ Nbd7 Vaganian+Agzamov, Game 51, saw White

obtain a clear edge after 7...Bd7, e.g., 8.a4 O-O 9.O-O Na6
10.Bxa6 bxa6 11.b3 Bf5 12.Nd2 Nd7 13.Nc4 Bf6 14.Bb2 Nb6
15.Ne3 Bg6 16.Qd2 Re8 17.a5. **8.a4 O-O 9.O-O a6** 9...Ne8
was tried in Trofimov/Psakhis, Leningrad 1979, with the fol-
lowup: 10.Re1 Nc7 11.Bf4 a6 12.Bc4 Re8 13.Qd3 Nf8 14.h3
Ng6 15.Bh2 Rb8 (15...b6 was better) 16.a5 b5 17.axb6 Rxb6
18.Na4 Rb7 19.Re3 and White was better. **10.Be2 b6 11.Re1
Re8 12.Bf4** White develops his bishop in classical fashion,
attacking the d6-pawn. **12...Nf8** >...Ng6; Black tries to find a
more active square for this knight, which is clogging his piece
development. Note that 12...Nf8 is made possible by deferring
the natural bishop retreat, ...Bf8. This maneuver will be re-
peated in Game 48: Gligoric=Larsen, Busum 1969. **13.h3 Ng6
14.Bh2 Bf8 15.Bd3 Rxe1+ 16.Qxe1 Bb7 17.Qd2** Tactical
defense; if 17...Nxd5? 18.Nxd5 Bxd5 19.Bxg6 Bxf3 20.Bxh7+!
Kxh7 21.Qd3+. **17...Qd7 18.Bc4 Qf5 19.Re1 Re8** 19...Ne7?
20.Bxd6! **20.Rxe8 Nxe8 21.Qe2 Nc7 22.Qe4 Qf6 23.h4 Bc8?!**
23...Ne7 was better, keeping up the pressure on d5 and preparing to counter 24.Ng5 with 24...g6. **24.Bd3!** Now Black is
forced to weaken the pawn cover around his king. **24...h5** The
alternative, 24...Be7 25.h5 Nf8, was passive and unappetizing.
25.Nd1 b5 26.axb5 axb5 27.c3 c4 28.Bc2 28.Bb1 was preferable. **28...Bd7 29.Ne3 Na6 30.Bg3 Nc5 31.Qd4 Qd8**

32.Ng5? The paradoxical move 32.Qd1!, with a latent (but
potent) attack against the h5-pawn, would have given White
the better game. For reasons perhaps grounded in chess
psychology, it is often difficult to find strong moves which
require the retreat of a well-posted piece. **32...Be7 33.f4 Bf6
34.Qd2** And now it is too late to employ the Qd1 idea:

34.Qd1? Qe7 35.Kf2 (35.Qf3 Nd3!) 35...Bxg5 36.fxg5 Ne4+!, and if 37.Bxe4 Qxe4 38.Qxh5 Nf4 39.Qf3 (39.Bxf4 Qxf4+ 40.Ke2 g6 41.Qh6 Bg4+!) 39...Nd3+. **34...Qe7 35.Nf5 Bxf5 36.Bxf5 Nf8 37.Bf2 Na4 38.g3 g6 39.Bb1 Nd7 40.Nf3 Ndc5 -+ 41.Bxc5? Nxc5 42.Kg2 Qa7!** With this sudden shift to the a-file, White's queen-side becomes completely indefensible. **43.f5 Qa1 44.Bc2 Qxb2 45.fxg6 fxg6 46.Qe2 Kg7 47.Nd4 Be5 48.Qe3 Nd3 49.Qg5 Bxd4** White Resigns.

Game 48: Gligoric=Larsen, Busum 1969

1.d4 e6 2.e4 c5 3.d5 exd5 4.exd5 d6 5.Nf3 Nf6 6.Bb5+ Nbd7 7.O-O Be7 after 7...a6 8.Re1+ Be7 9.Bf1 b5, White, having omitted Nc3, can counter Black's queen-side expansion with 10.a4! **8.a4** Bohm+Johansen, Game 49, saw White directly reinforce his d5-pawn after 8.Re1 a6 9.Bf1 O-O 10.a4 b6 11.c4. **8...O-O 9.Re1 Re8 10.Nc3 a6 11.Bf1** White tucks his bishop away on this square so that it does not block the e-file, obstruct the defense of d5, or become a target on c4. **11...b6** To make ...b5 possible should White play a5. **12.b3** Since Black can adequately defend the backward pawn at d6, White seeks to maximize the activity of his dark-squared bishop. **12...Nf8** Freeing up his pieces and heading for g6. **13.Bb2 Bb7 14.Bc4** Since Black's current piece placement makes ...b5 difficult to achieve, White feels justified in redeploying the bishop to c4. **14...Ng6** The position is roughly balanced. **15.Ne4 Nxe4 16.Rxe4 Bf8** 16...Bf6? 17.Rxe8+ Qxe8 Bxf6 +-. **17.Rxe8** 17.Qd3 immediately may be better. **17...Qxe8 18.Qd3** If 18.Qf1, Black can play 18...Qe4! **18...b5!**

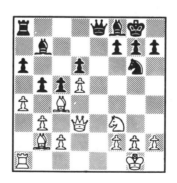

76

There is a clever tactical justification for this in Black's 21st move. **19.axb5 axb5 20.Bxb5 Rxa1+ 21.Bxa1 Qa8** With this double attack on the Ba1 and the d5-pawn, Black regains material equality. **22.Bc3 Bxd5 23.Qe3 Qa2 24.Ne1 Be6 25.Qc1 Qa8 26.Qa1 Qb8 27.Bf1 d5 28.g3 h5?** Overly optimistic. The advanced pawn becomes a weakness instead of a threat. **29.Qd1! d4 30.Bd2 Qe5 31.Nf3 Qf6 32.Ng5 Bg4 33.Be2 Ne5 34.Bf4?** White misses his chance to cut off support to the Bg4 with 34.f4!, e.g., 34...d3 35.cxd3 Bxe2 (If 35...Nxd3, 36.Be3! wins a pawn) 36.Qxe2 Ng4 37.h3 Qa1+ 38.Kg2 Nf6 39.Ne4 leaves White a solid pawn up. **34...g6!** Now the pawn on h5 is defended and 35.Bxe5 Qxe5 36.Bxg4 can be answered by 36...Qxg5. **35.Bxe5 Qxg5** Larsen characteristically tries for more, avoiding the opposite-colored bishop endgame after 35...Qxe5. **36.Bf4 Qf5 37.f3 Bh3 38.Bc4 g5 39.Bc1 Bg7 40.Bd3 Qd5 41.Qe2** And here White offered a Draw which was accepted by Black, since after 41...Bf6! neither side can achieve much.

Game 49: Bohm+Johansen, Arnhem/Amsterdam 1983

1.d4 e6 2.e4 c5 3.d5 exd5 4.exd5 d6 5.Bb5+ Nd7 6.Nf3 Nf6 7.O-O Be7 8.Re1 a6 9.Bf1 A convenient place to warehouse the bishop and await developments. **9...O-O** Black refrains from 9...b5 since White has not yet committed his queen's knight. **10.a4 b6** Or else White plays a4-a5 and cripples Black's queen-side. **11.c4 Ne8** A critical juncture for Black. White's Bb5+ has left Black cramped, so he tries to untangle his pieces and find some counterplay. **12.Nc3 Nc7 13.Qc2 Nf6 14.Bd3 Re8** 14...Bg4!? was worth a try. **15.b3 Bd7** Black strives for ...b5, but White's attack is too swift. 15...Bf8 16.Rxe8 Ncxe8, intending ...Ra8-a7-e7 was a much better defense; if 17.Ng5, not 17...h6?? 18.Bh7+! Kh8 19.Nxf7+ but rather 17...g6. **16.Ng5 h6?**

(See the diagram on the top of the next page)

16...g6. **17.Bh7+ Kf8 18.Nxf7! Kxf7 19.Qg6+ Kf8 20.Bxh6! gxh6 21.Qxh6+ Kf7 22.Bg6+ Kg8 23.Ne4 Ncxd5 24.cxd5** Black Resigns.

Game 50: Karner=Suba, Tallinn 1983

1.d4 e6 2.e4 c5 3.d5 exd5 4.exd5 d6 5.Nc3 Nf6 6.Bb5+ Nbd7 7.a4 White ensures that if Black plays ...a6, kicking the Bb5, Black will not be able to immediately follow up with ...b5. **7...g6!?**

Instead of the customary 7...Be7, Black opts for a different developmental approach. Unlike Jamieson+Levy, Game 42, White has not developed his king's knight; therefore, Re1+, preventing Black from castling, is not a threat. Nonetheless, White can play Qe2+, which is equally disruptive. Black, however, is prepared for this. **8.Qe2+ Qe7!** Of course! With the queens off the board, White's attack will lose some of its sting and Black's cramp will be lessened. For a few moves, though, Black will undergo some defensive contortions due to the awkward position of his king. **9.Bg5 Bg7 10.Qxe7+ Kxe7 11.O-O-O a6 12.Re1+ Kd8 13.Bxd7 Kxd7** 13...Bxd7?? 14.Ne4! **14.a5!?** Preventing ...b5, right? **14...b5!** Anyway!

15.axb6 Bb7 16.Bxf6 The pressure on the d5 pawn, which is thematic to the Barcza-Larsen, prompts White to exchange; he will gain enough time after Black's forced reply to reinforce the d5 pawn by c2-c4. **16...Bxf6 17.Ne4 Bd8 18.c4 f5** Now Black simply threatens to get his pawn back with ...Bxb6, so White takes drastic measures to enliven the game. **19.Nxd6!? Kxd6 20.Re6+ Kd7 21.Nf3** In exchange for the sacrificed piece, White has two pawns (although the one on b6 will probably fall), one of which is a strong protected passer, control of the e-file (21...Re8?? is crushed by 22.Ne5+!), a strong entry square for the knight on e5, and the fact that Black's pieces are cramped and hard to develop. **21...a5 >...Ra6. 22.Rhe1 Rf8 23.Ne5+ Kc8 24.d6 Bxb6 25.Re7 Rd8 26.Nf7 Bxg2** Black sacrifices the exchange to break the attack. **27.Nxd8 Bxd8 28.Rxh7 Be4 29.h4 Ra6 30.f3 Bxf3 31.Re6 >32.d7+. 31...Rb6 32.Rxg6 Be4 33.Re6 Rb4 34.b3 Rb7 34...Rxb3?** is met by 35.Re8!, e.g., 35...Rb7 36.Rhh8 Rd7 37.h5! and wins. **35.Rxb7 Bxb7 36.Re5 Be4 37.h5 Kd7 38.Rxc5 Kxd6 39.Rb5 f4 40.Kd2 f3 41.Ke3 Bc6** Draw.

Game 51: Vaganian+Agzamov, USSR Ch. 1983

1.d4 Nf6 2.Nf3 c5 3.d5 e6 4.Nc3 d6 5.e4 exd5 6.exd5 Be7 7.Bb5+ Bd7 7...Nbd7 is better. **8.a4 O-O 9.O-O Na6**

10.Bxa6! White normally refrains from this capture, because Black gets good positional compensation, including a half-open b-file for his rook and the two bishops. What Black does not get here as readily is the flank deployment ...a6-a5 and ...Bc8-a6, because his bishop is already sitting on d7. **10...bxa6 11.b3 Bf5 12.Nd2 Nd7 13.Nc4 Bf6 14.Bb2 Nb6** This is a better way of confronting the Nc4 than 14...Ne5 15.Ne3, when White can play 16.f4. **15.Ne3 Bg6 16.Qd2 Re8 17.a5!** Driving away the knight and preventing counterplay based on ...c4, e.g., 17.Ncd1 Rc8!, intending ...c4 and ...Rc7-e7. **17...Nd7 18.Na4 Bxb2 19.Nxb2 Qf6 20.Nbc4 h5 21.Rae1 Qf4?** A more straightforward plan was 21...Re7 and 22...Rae8. **22.Qd1! Rad8 23.g3 Qf6 24.f4 Be4** Losing a pawn, but otherwise, the bishop is shut out of play and Black is quickly overrun: 24...h4? 25.f5 Bh7 26.Ng4! **25.Qxh5 Nf8 26.h3 Nh7 27.Rd1 Qc3 28.Qe2 Qb4 29.Qf2 f5** (The best try to entrench the bishop. If 29...Nf6, then 30.f5! **30.g4** Logically undermining the bishop's support. **30...fxg4 31.hxg4 Nf6 32.Qd2!** Forcing out Black's queen, since exchanging leaves White with a won ending. **32...Qb7 33.g5 Kf7?!** Bravery born of desperation. After 33...Nh5, the knight is quickly evicted: 34.Qh2 g6 35.f5! **34.gxf6 Rh8** Too late, Black sees the penalty for his anticipated 34...gxf6: 35.Qh2! Rh8? 36.Qxh8! Rxh8 37.Nxd6+. **35.Ng2 gxf6 36.Rf2 Rh3 37.Re2 f5 38.Re3 Rh6 39.Rg3 Rdh8 40.Qc3 R8h7** Cruel fate: if 40...Rh1+? 41.Kf2 Rxd1? 42.Rg7+! **41.Kf2 Qe7 42.Re1 Rh2 43.Nd2 Qh4 44.Nxe4 fxe4 45.Ke2** The king commences his orderly withdrawal to safety. **45...Qh5+ 46.Kd2 Qxd5+ 47.Kc1 Rh1 48.Qc4 Rxe1+ 49.Nxe1 Qxc4 50.bxc4 Kf6 51.Ng2 Rh1+ 52.Kd2 Rg1** 52...Ra1 53.Nh4 **53.Rg5 Rf1 54.Ke3 Rd1 55.c3** Black Resigns.

A short story:

Game 52: Pribyl=Gavrikov, Tallinn 1985

1.d4 e6 2.e4 c5 3.d5 exd5 4.exd5 d6 5.Nf3 Nf6 6.Bb5+ Nbd7 7.a4 Be7 8.O-O O-O 9.Re1 Rb8 10.Bf1 Re8 11.c4 Nf8 Draw.

Chapter 6: 1.e4 e6 2.d4 c5 3.d5 exd5 4.exd5 d6
5.Nc3 Nf6 6.Be2 Be7 7.Nf3:

White adopts the 'exact' move order   (avoiding ...Bg4) and/or desires to develop   his bishop at e2, in classical fashion (after   5.Nf3 Nf6 6.Be2 or 5.Nf3 Nf6 6.Nc3   Be7 7.Be2)

Game 53: Orbaan-Uhlmann, Wageningen 1957

1.e4 e6 2.d4 c5 3.d5 exd5 4.exd5 d6 5.Nf3 Nf6 6.Nc3 Be7 7.Be2 O-O 8.O-O a6 9.a4 b6 10.Nd2 Nbd7 11.Nc4 Ne5 As in Gligoric+Barcza, Game 38, Black allows White to create a passed pawn with 12.Nxe5 dxe5, since Black would then blockade the pawn with Nf6-e8-d6. **12.Ne3 Re8 13.f4 Ng6 14.Bd3 Bf8 15.Qf3 Ra7**

This rook lift highlights one of the positive features of an early ...a6, namely, after White's almost inevitable reply a4, Black can play ...b6 not only to forestall a4-a5 but also to permit the lateral development of the rook along the second rank. Here, of course, this maneuver is only possible because there is no Black knight at d7 or c7. **16.Bd2 Re7 17.Rfe1 Qc7 18.Qf1 Qb7 19.Kh1 Qa8 20.Rad1 Bb7** Uhlmann instructively regroups his forces to pressure the d5-pawn; the pawn advance ...b5 is also in the air. **21.Bc4 Qc8 22.Bd3 Nh5 23.g3 Nf6 24.Bf5 Qa8 25.Qd3 b5** And now, after provoking White to weaken his king-side, Black begins his queen-side play. **26.axb5 axb5 27.Ra1 Qb8 28.Bh3** 28.Nxb5 Nxd5 29.Nxd5 Rxe1+ 30.Rxe1 Rxe1+ 31.Bxe1 Bxd5+ 32.Qxd5 Qxb5,

threatening ...Qf1mate and ...Qxb2 **28...b4 29.Ncd1** 29.Ne2
Nxd5 30.Nxd5 Bxd5 31.Qxd5 Rxe2 is equally hopeless, so
White probably had to maroon his knight with 29.Na2, e.g.,
29...Qa8? 30.Nxb4 **29...Nxd5 30.Bg2 Nf6 31.Nf2 Bxg2+
32.Kxg2 Qb7+ 33.Kg1 d5 34.Qa6 Qxa6 35.Rxa6 d4 36.Ng2
Re2 37.Rd1 c4 38.f5 Ne5 39.Kf1 Nf3 40.Bf4 Rxc2** White
Resigns.

Game 54: Sandor+Barcza, Budapest 1960

**1.d4 e6 2.e4 c5 3.d5 exd5 4.exd5 d6 5.Nc3 Be7 6.Be2
Nf6 7.Nf3** White, an experienced Hungarian international
master, employs this move order to avoid Barcza's exchanging
maneuver ...Bc8-g4x(N)f3. **7...O-O 8.O-O Nbd7** The
idea ...Nb8-a6-c7 had not yet been discovered when this game
was played, three years after Barcza's modern interpretation of
the defense was introduced. **9.Re1 Re8 10.h3 Nf8 11.Nd2 Ng6
12.Nc4 Nd7 13.Bd3 Nde5 14.Bxg6 Nxg6** 14...Nxc4? loses a
pawn to 15.Bxh7+! Kxh7 16.Qd3+ followed by 17.Qxc4.
15.Nb5! Rf8 A sad necessity, but the d6-pawn has come under
heavy fire; if 15...a6?, White gladly moves the Nb5 with
16.Nbxd6!, and Black is embarrassed, because 16...Bxd6 is met
by 17.Rxe8+. **16.Bd2 b6** Again, ...a6 is wrong, but for a different reason: 16...a6? 17.Ba5! **17.a4 a6** Finally playable!
**18.Nc3 Bd7 19.Qh5! b5 20.axb5 axb5 21.Rxa8 Qxa8 22.Nb6
Qb7 23.Nxd7 Qxd7 24.Ne4 Qb7 25.Qf5 Nh4 26.Qh5 g6?**

Black would have done better to go for the draw by
repetition of position with 26...Ng6. The active try 26...f5?! is
met by 27.Ng5 Bxg5 28.Bxg5 Ng6 29.Qd1, and if 29...h6, then
30.Re6! Kh7 (30...Ne5 31.Bf4!) 31.Rxd6 hxg5 32.Qh5+ and

Qxg6 leaves White on top. **27.Qe2!** >27.Nxc5. **27...Qxd5?** After this, Black must lose the exchange. **28.Bh6!** With the insidious threat 28...R(any) 29.Nf6+ Bxf6 30.Qe8+ Rxe8 31.Rxe8 mate! **28...f5 29.Bxf8 Kxf8 30.g3** And not 30.Qd2?? Qa8! 31.Qh6+ Kg8 and White loses a piece. **30...Qxe4 31.Qxe4 fxe4 32.gxh4 Bxh4** 32...d5 33.Rd1 d4 34.Re1. **33.Rxe4 Bf6 34.b3 b4 35.Kg2 Kf7 36.f4! d5 37.Re2 Bc3 38.Kf3 Bd4?**

Here Black misses his best chance to hold the draw. With 38...Kf6!, Black could answer 39.Re8 with 39...h5!, and defend the White rook's attacks against the g6 and d5 pawns by shuttling his king about the e6, f6 and f5 squares. White's only real winning attempt would consist of the break f4-f5?!, which could easily backfire. **39.h4 Bf6** And now it's too late to play 39...Kf6: 40.h5! gxh5 41.Rh2 Kg6 42.Rg2+ Kf6 43.Rg5! **40.h5! gxh5 41.f5 c4 42.Rd2!** White must not relax; if he plays the 'natural' 42.bxc4, Black draws with the study-like 42...dxc4 43.Re4 b3! 44.Rxc4 b2 45.Rb4 h4! 46.Rb7+ Ke8 47.c4 Kd8 48.c5 Kc8 49.c6 h5! In this position, White is unable to make progress. His rook must keep the b2-pawn under constant surveillance, his king cannot wander away from the h4-pawn, and meanwhile Black can mark time with ...Kc8-d8-c8. **42...cxb3 43.cxb3 d4 44.Ke4 h4 45.Ra2! Kg7 46.Kd5 Kh6 47.Ke6 Bg5 48.f6 Kh5 49.Ra5 h3 50.f7 h2 51.Ra1!** Precise play! The careless 51.f8(Q) allows Black to escape with 51...h1(Q) 52.Qf7+ Kh6! **51...Bh6 52.Rh1 Bf8 53.Rxh2+ Kg4 54.Rd2** Black Resigns.

Game 55: Hamilton-Larsen, Lugano Olympiad 1968

1.d4 e6 2.e4 c5 3.d5 exd5 4.exd5 d6 5.Nc3 Nf6 6.Nf3 Be7 7.Be2 O-O 8.O-O Na6 Larsen was the first to consistently employ the knight development ...Nb8-a6-c7. **9.Bf4 Nc7 10.a4 b6 11.Bc4 a6 12.Qd3** This move is directed at hindering ...b5 as much as getting White's rooks connected. **12...Re8 13.Rab1?!** White is understandably concerned about falling behind in the battle for the queen-side, but this move, contemplating 14.b4, is too slow. **13...Qd7!** After 13...Bd7 14.b4 b5 15.axb5 axb5 16.Nxb5 Nxb5 17.Bxb5 Bxb5 18.Qxb5 Nxd5 19.Bd2, Black has few worries, but the text is more dynamic. **14.h3** White is faced with a dilemma, because before proceeding on the queen-side, he must take time to stop Black's tactical threats; if 14.b4 immediately, then 14...Qg4! e.g., 14.Bg3 Bf5 15.Qe2 Bf8! 16.h3 Rxe2 17.hxg4 Rxc2. **14...Qf5 15.Bg3 Qxd3 16.Bxd3 Bb7 17.Bc4 Bf8! 18.Rbd1** White must abandon his queen-side ambitions and resign himself to passive defense of the d5-pawn. **18...Bc8!**

Larsen (like any grandmaster) is never satisfied with his pieces' scope, and is constantly searching for more effective ways to utilize them. Here, Black has tied White down to defending the d5-pawn, but Larsen sees that White's task, though unpleasant, can certainly be accomplished satisfactorily. Therefore, it is time to shift the attack to new targets, such as the White pawn on c2. This constant probing for fresh weaknesses causes White's game to collapse. **19.Rfe1 Bf5 20.Rd2** An awkward defensive move necessitated by the potential energy of Black's queen-side; 20.Bb3? b5! **20...Rxe1 21.Nxe1 Re8 22.Kf1 Bd7** The bishop assumes a third role:

supporting ...b5. **23.Be2** If 23.Bh4 Ne4! **23...h6 24.Bf3 b5**
25.Re2? White cracks under the pressure, but 25.axb5 axb5
26.Ne2 Ne4 is tantamount to positional surrender. **25...b4**
26.Ne4 Nxe4 27.Rxe4 Bxa4 28.Ke2 Bb5+ 29.Kd2 Rxe4
30.Bxe4 Bc4 Coming full circle, the bishop concludes the game
in its initial function, attacking the d5-pawn. **31.Nd3 Bxd5**
32.Bf5 Ne6 33.b3 g6 34.Bg4 and White Resigns.

Game 56: Havasi-Titkos, Hungary 1969

1.e4 e6 2.d4 c5 3.d5 exd5 4.exd5 d6 5.Nc3 Nf6 6.Be2
Be7 7.Nf3 O-O 8.O-O Na6 9.Nb5?! One almost instinctively
feels that this rather artificial attempt to prevent ...Nc7 cannot
amount to much. **9...Bd7 10.c4** White reinforces the d5-pawn,
which is often a source of concern; however, the Be2's scope is
further limited. 10.a4 is another approach, tried in Tatai-
Quinteros, Game 67. **10...Bxb5 11.cxb5 Nc7 12.Bc4 a6**
13.bxa6 13.b6? Nce8 14.Qb3 Nd7 just loses a pawn. **13...b5!**
14.Be2 Rxa6 15.a4 Nfxd5 16.Bxb5 Nxb5 17.Qxd5 Nc7
18.Qd3 Bf6! Black stands better. **19.Ra2 Qd7 20.Ng5 Bxg5**
21.Bxg5 d5 22.Bf4 c4 23.Qc2 Ne6 24.Bd2 Rfa8 25.a5 Nd4!
26.Qa4?

24.Qd1 was necessary, but after 24...Nb3, White's game
was bad in any case. **26...Nf3+!! 27.gxf3 Rg6+ 28.Kh1 Qh3**
White Resigns.

Game 57: Diez del Corral+Fuller, Siegen Olympiad
1970

1.e4 e6 2.d4 c5 3.d5 exd5 4.exd5 d6 5.Nc3 Nf6 6.Be2

Be7 **7.Nf3 O-O 8.O-O b6?! 9.Nd2 Na6 10.Re1 Nc7 11.Nc4 Bb7 12.Bf3 Qd7** 12...Re8 looks better, and if 13.Bf4 Bf8 **13.Bf4 Rad8** White was threatening 14.Rxe7. **14.g4 h6 15.Ne3 Rfe8 16.h4 Qc8** Not to provide a retreat for the Nf6, but rather for the queen herself! 17.g5 hxg5 18.hxg5 Nh7 19.Bg4! was threatened. **17.g5 hxg5 18.hxg5 Nh7 19.Ne4 b5** Trying to forestall c2-c4, but White is able to open the a-file with great effect. **20.a4 Qa8 21.axb5 Nxd5 22.Nxd5 Bxd5 23.Ra3 Bb7 24.b6 d5?!**

24...a6 was ugly but necessary. **25.Rxa7!** Black will get rook, bishop and knight for his queen, but his resulting pieces will be in disarray. **26...Qxa7 26.bxa7 dxe4 27.Qe2 exf3 28.Qb5!** Highlighting the awkward positioning of the Black forces. **28...Ba8 29.Bd6 Kf8 30.Rxe7! Rxe7 31.Qxc5** 31.Qb8?! Rde8. **31...Rde8 32.Qf5!** Black Resigns. 32...Kg8 33.Bxe7 Rxe7 34.Qc8+ Nf8 35.Qxa8; 32...g6 33.Qe5!

Game 58: Rakic+Todorcevic, Vrnjacka Banja 1970

1.e4 e6 2.d4 c5 3.d5 exd5 4.exd5 d6 5.Nc3 Nf6 6.Be2 Be7 7.Nf3 a6 Black attempts to find something more active than 7...O-O, but since White answers ...a6 with a4 about 99 times out of 100 (unless White is a computer), Black is better off sticking to 'normal' developmental schemes. **8.a4 h6** Preparing a retreat for the Bc8 after ...Bf5, but this proves to be a fatal weakening of the king-side. **9.O-O Bf5 10.Nd2 Nbd7 11.f4 b6**

(See the diagram at the top of the next page)

12.g4! Bh7 13.g5 Ng8 14.Nc4 Rb8 15.Bg4 hxg5 16.fxg5 Ne5 17.Nxe5 dxe5 18.Qf3 Bg6 19.d6! Qxd6 20.Rd1 e4 21.Qf2 Qc7 22.Bf4 Qa7 23.Rd7 Rb7 24.Rd5 c4 25.Rad1 f5 26.Nxe4! fxe4 27.Bd7+ Rxd7 28.Rxd7 Qxd7 29.Rxd7 Kxd7 30.Qd4+ Ke6 31.Qxg7 Bc5+ 32.Kg2 Kf5 33.Qxh8 Kxf4 34.Qxg8 Kxg5 35.a5 e3 36.Qxc4 Bf5 37.axb6 Bxb6 38.h4+ Kh5 39.Qf4 Black Resigns.

Game 59: Unzicker-Larsen, Lugano 1970

1.d4 e6 2.e4 c5 3.d5 exd5 4.exd5 d6 5.Nc3 Nf6 6.Nf3 Be7 7.Be2 O-O 8.O-O Na6 9.Bf4 Nc7 10.Re1 b6 11.h3 Re8 12.a4 Bf8 13.Qd2 h6 Larsen waits. 13...h6 can be useful, inasmuch as it keeps White pieces (particularly a bishop) out of g5 and delays developing the Bc8 until White commits himself to a particular strategy. **14.Nh2** White recognizes the danger to the d5-pawn and decides to exchange off one of its attackers by playing his knight to g4, with Nxf6 in mind. While such a plan has some strategic merit, it does take time. **14...a6** 14...Bb7 is met by 15.Bf3. **15.Ng4 Bf5!** As in Hamilton-Larsen, Game 55, White adequately defends the d5-pawn, so Larsen finds the most active placement for his bishop. **16.Ne3** Although 16.Nxf6+ is consistent with White's plans, after 16...Qxf6 Black would threaten ...Qd4 (and, in some cases, ...Bxc2). 16.Ne3, however, does force the exchange of one pair of knights, since 16...Bg6 would allow White to play 17.Nc4. **16...Ne4 17.Nxe4 Bxe4** The bishop attacks the d5-pawn from a new square. **18.c4**

(See the diagram at the top of the next page)

White makes sure his d5-pawn will be immune to attack, but in so doing, he weakens the h7-b1 and g7-a1 diagonals; incidentally, the pawn moved to c4 becomes weak itself. If 18.Bd3? Qf6! wins a pawn, but Black must avoid 18.Bd3? Bxd3 19.Qxd3 Qf6 20.Bg3 Qxb2, because his queen becomes trapped after 21.c3! **18...Qf6 19.Bg3 Bg6** >...Re4; 19...h5!? was an enterprising alternative. **20.Bf1** 20.Ng4!? > Bd3. **20...h5 21.Rad1 Rb8** Black, with good prospects of active queen-side counter-play, is slightly better. **22.b3 b5 23.axb5** White would prefer not to assist Black's plan, but ...bxa4, followed by ...Rb4 attacking the split pawns, was threatened. **23...axb5 24.Bd3 bxc4 25.Bxg6 Qxg6** But not 25...c3? because of 26.Bxf7+. **26.bxc4 Na6** Black gets his poorly-placed knight into play. **27.Nf1** Up to this point, White had been holding on to his position, despite Black's slightly superior piece activity. The text envisions exchanging off the rooks along the e-file. But 27.Nf1 seems to miss the point of Black's last move. Since Black is clearly planning to play Na6-b4, White should have played 27.Nc2 instead, contemplating the exchange of knights, as well as the rooks. **27...Nb4 28.Rxe8 Rxe8 29.Ne3?!** A time-trouble error that causes further difficulties for White. 29.Re1 was better, e.g., 29...Rxe1 30.Qxe1 Qc2 31.Qe8! > Bxd6. Black's best would be to disdain the rook trade with 29...Ra8!, maintaining his superior piece activity. **29...Qe4!** Black's queen becomes much more powerful through this centralization. **30.Ra1 g6 31.h4 Qd4!** The exchange of queens only helps Black. **32.Rd1?!** 32.Qxd4 cxd4 33.Nf1, painful as it might be, was the last, albeit futile, hope. **32...Qxd2 33.Rxd2 Re4!** A hammer blow that highlights all of White's weaknesses: the pawns on h4 and c4, awkward piece placement (in the face of ...f7-f5-f4), and susceptibility to ...Rd4 (if Rxd4, ...cxd4

creates a passed pawn and chases the knight.) White is lost.
34.Rd1 f5 >35...f4. **35.Nf1 Rxc4 36.f3 Be7 37.Kh2 Kf7 38.Rd2 Rd4 39.Rxd4 cxd4 40.Nd2 Nxd5** White Resigns.

Game 60: Portisch+Barcza, Budapest 1972

1.d4 e6 2.e4 c5 3.d5 exd5 4.exd5 d6 5.Nf3 Be7 6.h3 White radically prevents ...Bg4, but is such prophylaxis really necessary? Barcza was known to favor ...Bg4, and there's something to be said for denying one's opponent familiar terrain, but Black could have played 5...Bg4 if that was in fact his intention. Portisch, however, subsequently finds a way to give 6.h3 meaning. **6...a6 7.a4 Nf6 8.Nc3 b6 9.Bc4 Nbd7 10.O-O O-O** The familiar maneuver ...Ne5, intending to place a blockading knight at d6, does not work here: 10...Ne5? 11.Nxe5 dxe5 12.Re1 Qc7 13.Qe2 Nd7 14.f4! and White is winning. **11.Re1 Bb7?!** 11...Re8. **12.Qe2 Re8 13.Qd3** Still deterring ...b5. **13...Nf8 14.Bf4 Ng6 15.Bh2 Bf8 16.Ng5 Bc8** 16...h6 was better. **17.f4! Qd7 18.g4!**

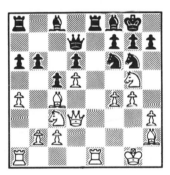

not in chessmax.com

White prevents 18...Qf5 and further cramps Black; 19.f4-f5 is now threatened so Black must squirm to create a retreat for his Ng6. **18...Rxe1+ 19.Rxe1 Be7 20.f5 Nf8 21.Qe3 Ra7 22.Nf3 h6 23.Bf1 N8h7 24.Nd2 Qd8 25.Bg2 Bf8 26.Qf4!** Ne8 26...Re7 27.Rxe7 Bxe7 28.Nc4 Ne8 29.Ne4! **27.Nc4 Nhf6 28.h4 Re7 29.Rf1 h5 30.g5 Ng4 31.Bg3 Rd7 32.Bf3 b5 33.axb5 axb5 34.Nxb5 Ba6 35.Bxg4 hxg4** 35...Bxb5 36.Bxh5. **36.Nc3 Bxc4 37.Qxc4 Rb7 38.Qxg4 Rxb2 39.Ne4! Qd7 40.Qh5 g6 41.fxg6 fxg6 42.Qxg6+ Bg7 43.Nf6+ Nxf6 44.gxf6 c4 45.f7+** Black Resigns.

Game 61: Barreras=Jimenez, Cienfuegos 1972

1.e4 e6 2.d4 c5 3.d5 exd5 4.exd5 d6 5.Nc3 Nf6 6.Be2 Be7 7.Nf3 O-O 8.O-O a6 9.a4 Re8 10.Re1 Bf8 11.Bg5 h6 12.Bh4 g5!? 13.Bg3 Nh5 14.Bd3 Rxe1+ 15.Qxe1 Nxg3 16.hxg3 Nd7 17.Ne4 Qe7 Draw. It's a shame the combatants agreed to a cessation of hostilities, because it would be interesting to see if Black's two bishops could provide adequate compensation for his weakened king-side.

Game 62: Moiseev+Bitman, Moscow Ch. Semi-Final 1972

1.e4 e6 2.d4 c5 3.d5 exd5 4.exd5 d6 5.Nc3 Nf6 6.Be2 Be7 7.Nf3 O-O 8.O-O b6?! 9.Nd2 Bb7 10.Nc4 Na6 11.Bf4 Nc7 12.Ne3 Qd7 13.a4 a6 14.g4!

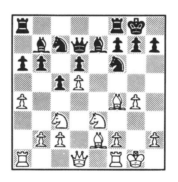

A logical, space-gaining thrust. White's king-side may be weakened, but Black is in no position to take advantage of this. 14...h6 15.h4 Qd8 16.Bg3 Nfe8 Might as well leave before asked to do so. 17.Nf5 Bc8 Hoping for 18...Bxf5. 18.Nxe7+ Qxe7 19.Qd2 f5 20.g5 hxg5 21.hxg5 f4?! Black makes a speculative sacrifice to activate his pieces, but dour defense with 21...g6 and ...Rf7-h7 was required. 22.Bxf4 Qf7 23.Bg3 Rb8 24.Rfe1 Rb7 25.Bf1 b5 26.axb5 axb5 27.Bg2 Bf5 28.Re2 b4 29.Nd1 Nb5 >30...Nd4. 30.c3 Qh5 31.Ra8 Bg4 32.Re1 Bxd1 33.Qxd1 Qxd1 34.Rxd1 bxc3 35.bxc3 Nxc3 Black has restored material equality, but White's two bishops are just too powerful. 36.Re1 Rb1 37.Rxb1 Nxb1 38.Bh3 Nc3 39.Be6+ Kh7 40.Bd7 Ne2+ 41.Kg2 Nxg3 42.Kxg3 Kg6 There is no salvation in 42...Nf6, e.g., 43.Bf5+ Kg8 44.Rxf8+ Kxf8

45.gxf6. **43.Rxe8 Rxe8 44.Bxe8+ Kxg5 45.Kf3 Kf5 46.Ke3 Ke5 47.Bf7 g5 48.Be6 Kf6 49.Ke4 Kg6 50.Bg4 Kf6 51.Bh5** Black Resigns.

Game 63: Rossetto-Hubner, Skopje Olympiad 1972

1.d4 Nf6 2.Nc3 c5 3.d5 d6 4.Nf3 e6 5.e4 exd5 6.exd5 Be7 7.h3?! This absolute prevention of ...Bg4 is unnecessary, since after 7.Be2 Bg4?! White has 8.Nd2! **7...O-O 8.Bf4** White deferred this bishop's development in Goldin/Konstantinopolpolsky, USSR 1976, and instead played 8.Bd3. After 8...b6?! (8...a6 9.a4 Bd7, intending ...Rb8 and ...b5 may be better) 9.O-O Na6 10.Re1 Nc7 11.Bf4 Bb7 12.Bc4 Qd7 13.Qd3 a6 14.a4 h6 15.Nh4! Bc8 16.Nf5! Re8 17.Nxe7+ Rxe7 18.Rxe7 Qxe7 19.Qg3 Nce8 20.Bxh6, White had an extra pawn and a much better game. **8...b6** Black could just as well have played 8...Na6; 9.Bxa6 bxa6 10.Nd2 > 11.Nc4 is roughly balanced. **9.Bc4?** 9.Be2 is simpler, since on c4 the bishop may become exposed to a Black queen-side pawn advance. **9...Na6 10.O-O Nc7 11.Re1 a6 12.a4 Rb8 13.Qe2 Re8 14.Rad1 Qd7 15.Ba2?** It was too early to retreat. 15.b3 b5 16.axb5 axb5 17.Bd3 was more solid. **15...b5 16.axb5 axb5 17.Qd2** White must tread lightly: 17.Ne4, trying to exchange off one of the harrassing knights, is effectively answered by 17...Bb7, and 17.Ng5, intending the sacrificial leap Ne6, is simply unsound. **17...Bb7 18.Ne4**

18...Nxe4 Now it is Black's turn to be careful. The hasty 18...Ncxd5? completely dissipates Black's advantage after 19.Bxd6! (A similar combination can be found in D. Gurevich=Kavalek, Game 73) 19...Bxd6 20.Nxf6+ Nxf6 21.Qxd6 Bxf3 22.Qxd7 Rxe1+ 23.Rxe1 Nxd7 24.gxf3; and 18...Nfxd5

leads to a murky situation after 19.Bg3. Hubner eschews the d5-pawn until he can weaken it further. **19.Rxe4 Ra8 20.Bb1 Nxd5** Now the time is right! **21.c3 g6 22.Bg3 Nb6 23.Rg4?** An over-optimistic sortie that simply loses the exchange, but White was hard-pressed to find a good rook move: 23.Re2 Bxf3 24.gxf3 Qxh3 25.Rde1 Qd7 leaves Black two pawns up with the better position. **23...Bxf3 24.gxf3 f5!** It's all over. The position of the Rg4 is tragi-comical. **25.Rg5 Bxg5 26.Qxg5 d5 27.b4 c4 28.Kg2 Qg7 29.Bd6 Na4 30.Bc5 Nxc5 31.bxc5 Qe5 32.h4 Ra3 33.h5 Qxc3 34.Qg3 Qe5 35.hxg6 Qxg3+ 36.Kxg3 hxg6 37.Rxd5 Rc8** White Resigns.

Game 64: Browne=Evans, San Antonio 1972

1.e4 e6 2.d4 c5 3.d5 exd5 4.exd5 d6 5.Nc3 Nf6 6.Nf3 Be7 7.Be2 O-O 8.Nd2 Na6 9.Nc4 Nc7 10.a4 b6 11.O-O Bb7 12.Bf3 White is content to undertake a simple, solid defense of his d5-pawn and await developments. **12...Qd7 13.Bf4 Rfe8 14.Qd3 h6** This preparation for ...Bf8 prevents White from playing Bf4-g5x(N)f6, destroying Black's king-side pawns. **15.Bg3 Bf8 16.Rfd1 Ba6**

17.b3 Ng4 >18...Ne5. **18.Re1** White initiates a series of exchanges that end in sterile equality. **18...Rxe1+ 19.Rxe1 Re8 20.Rxe8 Qxe8 21.Qe4 Nf6 22.Qxe8 Nfxe8 23.Ne3 g6 24.h4 h5 25.Ne4** Draw.

Game 65: Balashov+Savon, USSR Ch. Semi-Final 1974

1.e4 e6 2.d4 c5 3.d5 exd5 4.exd5 d6 5.Nc3 Nf6 6.Be2

Be7 7.Nf3 O-O 8.O-O b6?! Looks natural; if Black intends to play ...Na6 anyway, what difference does it make if he plays ...b6 first? Plenty! To see why, look at Chandler+Mikh. Tseitlin, Game 75. **9.Nd2** 9.Re1! **9...Na6 10.Nc4 Nc7 11.Re1 Rb8 12.a4 a6 13.Bf3 Re8 14.h3 Bf8 15.Bf4 Rxe1+ 16.Qxe1 Nce8 17.Nd1 Bf5** With White's c2-pawn undefended, Black can develop this piece to f5 with tempo, unafraid of g2-g4. **18.Qe2 Qe7 19.Nde3 Bg6 20.c3 h6 21.Re1 Qd7** Ensuring ...b5, so White finds a way to make a nuisance of his Nc4. **22.a5 b5 23.Nb6 Qd8 24.b4 c4 25.Nc2 Bd3 26.Qd2 Bxc2** Black has to prevent Nc2-d4-c6. **27.Qxc2 Nd7 28.Nxd7 Qxd7 29.Qd2 Be7 30.Re3 Bf6 31.Qe2 Qd8 32.Bh5 Kf8 33.Qc2 Kg8 34.Qe4 Qd7**

35.Bd1! Bg5 36.Bxg5 hxg5 37.Bg4 Qd8 38.Qe7! And White, having seized control of the seventh rank, went on to win.

Game 66: Navojan+Hachaturian, Armenian Ch. 1976

1.e4 e6 2.d4 c5 3.d5 exd5 4.exd5 d6 5.Nc3 Nf6 6.Be2 Be7 7.Nf3 O-O 8.O-O Bg4 9.a4 9.Nd2! **9...Nbd7 10.h3 Bh5?!** Black should shed his bad bishop with 10...Bxf3. **11.Bf4 a6** 11...Bxf3. **12.Nd2** White finally plays this thematic maneuver, compelling the exchange of bishops and heading for c4 with the knight. **12...Bxe2 13.Qxe2 Re8 14.a5 Bf8 15.Qf3 Ne5 16.Bxe5 dxe5 17.Rfe1 Bd6 18.Nc4 Qc7 19.Re2 Re7 20.Rae1 Rae8 21.g4 h6 22.h4 e4?! 23.Nxe4 Bh2+ 24.Kf1 Nxd5 25.Qf5 Nf4 26.Re3 Re5?!**

(See the diagram at the top of the next page)

Black, encouraged by the exposed position of White's queen, plays to trap her. **27.Nxe5 Rxe5 28.Ng5!** A nasty surprise! **28...Ng6** And now, Black sees, to his regret, that 28...Rxf5?? fails immediately to 29.Re8 mate! **29.Rxe5 Bxe5 30.h5 hxg5 31.hxg6 f6 32.Qe6+ Kf8 33.Rd1** Black Resigns. White's threat of Rd8+ cannot be parried; 33...Bd4 34.c3; 33...Qe7 34.Rd8+ Qxd8 35.Qf7mate.

Game 67: Tatai-Quinteros, Amsterdam 1977

1.e4 e6 2.d4 c5 3.d5 exd5 4.exd5 d6 5.Nc3 Nf6 6.Be2 Be7 7.Nf3 O-O 8.O-O Na6 9.Nb5 The same plan as seen in Havasi-Titkos, Game 56. **9...Bd7 10.a4** Not really an improvement over 10.c4 as in Havasi-Titkos. Although it does not obstruct the Be2 as much, Black's next move practically forces White to play c4 anyway. **10...Nb4 11.c4** After 11.Bc4 a6 12.Na3?! (12.Nc3 allows the Nb4 to remain in place without worry of c2-c3, but would be better.) 12...b5! 13.axb5 axb5 14.Ba2 (14.Bxb5?? Bxb5!) c4! -+, e.g., 15.b3?? Nxa2! 16.Rxa2 b4. **11...Bf5 12.Ne1 Qd7 13.h3 Rfe8 14.Ra3 a6 15.Nc3 Bg6 16.g4?! Ne4!**

2 moves missing

Black's knight leap shows that White's 16th move only amounted to a weakening of the king-side. **17.Ng2 Bf6 18.Nf4 Bd4 19.Nxg6 hxg6 20.Nxe4 Rxe4 21.Bf3 Re7** Black will double rooks and assume control of the open e-file, aided by the offside position of the Ra3. **22.a5 Rae8 23.Qb3 b5** Another demonstration of Black's ability to play ...b5 when a cursory examination of the position might indicate such an advance is infeasible; the Nb4 anchors the defense of the subsequently weakened a6-pawn, and the Black queen smoothly slides over to regain the material. **24.axb6 Qb7 25.Bd2 Qxb6 26.Bc3 Rb8 27.Qd1 a5 28.Qd2 Rbe8 29.Rfa1 Ra8 30.Ra4 Raa7 31.Kg2 Be5 32.Re1 Bf6 33.Be4 Qd8 34.g5 Qe8! 35.gxf6 Rxe4 36.fxg7? Rxe1 37.Qh6** And now White sees that his combinative hallucination proves his undoing after 37.Qxe1 Qxa4. **37...Qe4+ 38.f3 Qe2+ 39.Kg3 Rg1+** White Resigns. 40.Kh4 Qf2 mate; 40.Kf4 Nd3 mate.

Game 68: Vaganian+ L. Bronstein, Sao Paulo 1977

1.d4 e6 2.e4 c5 3.d5 exd5 4.exd5 d6 5.Nf3 Nf6 6.Nc3 Be7 7.Be2 O-O 8.O-O Na6 9.Re1 Nc7 10.a4 b6 11.Rb1 White opts for a different plan involving direct play on the queen-side. **11...Re8 12.h3 h6 13.Bc4 Bf8**

Since the publication of ECO vol. A in 1979, Vaganian+ L. Bronstein has been regarded by theory as one of White's best continuations; after 13...Bf8, White is considered to have a slight edge. In the little-known game Bohm-Konikowski, Dortmund II 1981, Game 70, Black found an improvement with 13...a6! which may cause this theoretical judgment to be reconsidered. **14.Rxe8 Qxe8 15.Be3** An excellent post for this piece; not only does it negate Black's influence along the e-file, it also can actively participate in White's queen-side play. **15...Bd7 16.b4! Ne4 17.Nxe4 Qxe4 18.Nd2 Qg6** With the undisguised threat of 19...Bxh3. **19.Bd3 Bf5 20.Bxf5 Qxf5 21.c4 Re8?!**

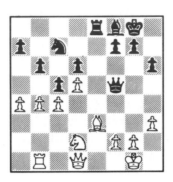

21...Na6!? 22.bxc5 dxc5, intending ...Nb4 and ...Bd6, might have been the best defensive attempt. If 21...Ne8, trying for a blockade on d6 after 22.bxc5 dxc5, White could play 23.Qb3, and a4-a5 would be a constant threat. **22.Qg4 Qc2 23.bxc5!** White's potential pawn advance is so strong that he can afford to sacrifice two pieces for Black's rook. **23...Rxe3 24.fxe3 Qxd2 25.c6 Qxe3+ 26.Kh1 Qe7 27.a5 h5 28.Qd7!** Black Resigns.

Game 69: Balashov=Kasparov, USSR Ch. 1979

1.d4 e6 2.e4 c5 3.d5 exd5 4.exd5 d6 5.Nc3 Nf6 6.Be2 Be7 7.Nf3 O-O 8.O-O Na6 9.h3 Rakitin/Schmid, Riga 1978 saw 9.Nd2 Nc7 10.Bf3 b5 11.Nde4 Bb7 12.Nxc5 dxc5 13.d6 Bxf3 14.dxe7 Bxd1 15.exd8(Q) Raxd8 16.Nxd1 Ne6, and Black was slightly better. **9...Nc7 10.Nh2** Not the most aggressive approach at White's disposal. 10.Nh2, however, is a fairly solid, positionally-based move, since White can either exchange off one of the d5-pawn's tormentors by Ng4 and Nxf6, or redeploy the knight to e3, as in the present game. Nevertheless, 10.Nd2, intending Nc4, is a more active plan. **10...a6 11.a4 b6 12.Ng4 Bb7 13.Ne3** 13.Nxf6+ Bxf6 14.Bf3 is dull but equal. White is content to simply overprotect the d5-pawn and play it safe. **13...Re8 14.Rb1 Bf8 15.b4**

15...cxb4 Kasparov's forthcoming combination could be played here as well: 15...Ncxd5 16.Nexd5 Nxd5 17.Nxd5 Bxd5 18.Be3 Bc6 19.bxc5 bxc5. **16.Rxb4 Ncxd5 17.Nexd5 Nxd5 18.Nxd5 Bxd5 19.Be3! Be4 20.Bxb6 Qg5 21.Rxe4** A 'drawing combination'. **21...Rxe4** Draw. 22.Bf3 wins back the exchange, resulting in sterile equality.

Game 70: Bohm-Konikowski, Dortmund II 1981

1.e4 e6 2.d4 c5 3.d5 exd5 4.exd5 d6 5.Nf3 Nf6 6.Nc3 Be7 7.Be2 O-O 8.O-O Na6 9.Re1 Nc7 10.a4 b6 11.Rb1 Re8 12.h3 h6 13.Bc4 a6! The aforementioned improvement over Vaganian+L. Bronstein, Game 68. Black defers ...Bf8, avoiding a rook exchange along the e-file, until White's intentions clarify. Meanwhile, Black will play ...Bd7 and simply threaten to expand on the queen-side. **14.b4 Bd7 15.bxc5 bxc5 16.Qd3** If 16.a5 (intending Nc3-a4-b6), Black has a strong move in 16...Nb5! **16...Qc8!** A nice move that keeps control over b7 and a6 while forming a Q+B battery that menaces ...Bf5. **17.Bf4 Bf5 18.Qd2 Bf8** Black now encourages the exchange of rooks along the e-file, since it enables him to obtain a queen-side initiative. **19.Rxe8 Qxe8 20.Re1 Qd7 21.Nh2 Re8 22.Rxe8 Qxe8 23.f3** Prevents 23...Ne4. **23...Qb8** Controlling the b-file and dominating the queen-side. **24.g4 Bg6 25.Nf1 Qb4!** Clearly demonstrating White's main weakness: awkward piece placement; now if 26.Bb3?? Qxf4. **26.Ne3**

(See the diagram at the top of the next page)

26...Ncxd5! 27.Nexd5 The Nc3 is pinned and 27.Bxd5 is met by 27...Qxf4. **27...Qxc4 28.Nxf6+ gxf6 29.Nd5 Qxa4 30.Nxf6+**

Kh8 31.Bxh6 Bg7! 32.Bxg7+ Kxg7 33.Ne8+? White's c2-pawn is under fire and even 33.Nh5+ loses; e.g., 33...Bxh5 34.gxh5 Qd4+! 35.Qxd4 cxd4 36.Kf1 a5 37.Ke1 a4 38.Kd2 a3 39.Kc1 Kh6 40.Kb1 Kxh5 41.Ka2 Kh4 42.Kxa3 Kxh3 43.Kb4 Kg3 44.Kc4 Kxf3 45.Kxd4 Kg4 46.Kd5 f5 47.Kxd6 f4 48.c4 f3 49.c5 f2 50.c6 f1(Q) 51.c7 Qf5!, but only by one tempo! **33...Qxe8** White Resigns.

Game 71: Velimirovic+Cebalo, Yugoslavia Ch. 1981

1.e4 e6 2.d4 c5 3.d5 exd5 4.exd5 d6 5.Nf3 Nf6 6.Be2 Be7 7.O-O O-O 8.Nc3 In Campora/Cebalo, Vrsac 1981, White played 8.Re1 Re8 9.c4, and after 9...Nbd7 10.Nc3 Nf8 11.h3 Bf5 12.Bf1 Ng6 13.Nh2 h6 14.g4 Bd7 15.f4 was slightly better, since his advantage in space compensated for his weakened king-side. **8...Na6** If 8...Bg4, 9.Nd2! **9.a3?!** This direct preparation for b4 is less flexible than Rb1 (which must be played anyway); White is better off playing a4 (often compelling ...b6) , Rb1 and b4 in that order. **9...Nc7 10.b4 b6 11.bxc5 bxc5 12.Rb1** Persuasive evidence that White has effectively wasted a tempo. **12...h6** Waiting. Here Black had an alternative in 12...Bf5 13.Bd3 Bg4 (not 13...Nfxd5? 14.Nxd5 Nxd5 15.Bxf5 Nc3 16.Qd3 Nxb1 17.Bb2! +-) 14.h3 Bh5 (Here, the exchange 14...Bxf3 15.Qxf3 is less desirable, since White's light-squared bishop is active and he controls the queen-side.) 15.g4! Bg6 16.Bxg6 hxg6 (16...fxg6!?), although after 17.Bf4 White would have the more comfortable game. **13.h3 Re8 14.Nh2!?** This maneuver, intending Ng4 and the exchange of the Nf6, has been seen before. White had to be wary of tactical tricks here: 14.Bf4 Bf5 15.Bd3? is answered by 15...Nfxd5! winning a pawn. A better move for White would be 15.Rb7.

14...Bf8 15.Ng4 Bxg4! Since the bishop is often exchanged for White's knight when the latter is on f3, this analogous approach seems a good idea in the present position, too, since ...Bb7 is impossible, and 15...Bf5 could be met by 16.Nxf6+ >17.g4. **16.hxg4** 16.Bxg4 is possibly stronger. **16...Rb8 17.Rxb8 Qxb8 18.f4?!**

18.Bf3 can be countered by 18...Nd7 > ...Ne5. White is stuck for a clear plan and so chooses the most obvious strategy: grabbing space. However, this meets with a simple tactical refutation. **18...Nfxd5! 19.Nxd5 Nxd5 20.Bf3** 20.Qxd5? Rxe2. **20...Nb6 21.Qd3 d5!?** Rather than suffer through a dour pawn-up defense with a backward d6-pawn, Black gives back his material gain to enhance his piece activity. **22.Bxd5 Rd8 23.c4 Nxd5 24.cxd5 Qc8!** Black eyes the weak g4-pawn, but, more important, puts a heavy piece behind his passed pawn. **25.Qf3 c4 26.Rd1** White follows suit. **26...Qc5+ 27.Kh2 c3 28.Rd3 Rc8 29.Qe4 Bd6!?** Tempting, since it activates the sleeping bishop and indirectly menaces White's king, but 29...c2! would have preserved Black's edge by forcing White to continually deal with tactics surrounding the queening threat. **30.g5! Qc4!** There is no time for 30...hxg5, because after 31.Rh3 g6 (31...c2 32.Qh7+ Kf8 33.Qh8+ Ke7 34.Qxg7) 32.Be3! (with the nasty threat 33.Bd4) White has a very strong attack. **31.Rd4 Qf1 32.g6!**

(See the diagram at the top of the next page)

Disregarding Black's threat. **32...Rf8!** The bishop could not be taken: 32...Qxc1?! 33.gxf7+ Kf8 (33...Kh8? 34.Qe8+!) 34.Qh7 Bxf4+ 35.g3 Bxg3+ 36.Kg2! (36.Kxg3? Qe3+) and

White has a roaring attack. **33.gxf7+ Kh8 34.Be3** If 34.Qe6, Black can play 34...Qxc1, e.g., 35.Qxd6 Rxf7. **34...Rxf7 35.Rc4! Qe1!** >36...Rxf4!! 37.Bxf4 Qxe4 38.Rxe4 Bxf4+ and 39...c1(Q). **36.Kh3 Rf8 37.Qe6 Rf6 38.Rc8+ Bf8 39.Qe7?** After 39.Qe4, it's anybody's game. **39...Kg8?** At this point, with both players in severe time-trouble, Black misses the win. The game was his after 39...Qh1+ 40.Kg3 Rg6+ 41.Kf2 Rxg2+ 42.Kf3 Qh3+ 43.Ke4 Qxc8. **40.Bc5?** White reciprocates! Of course, 40.Kh2 loses to 40...Qh4+ 41.Kg1 Qg4, but with 40.Qe4 (Again!) White could have kept the issue in doubt. **40...Qxe7??** It is sad but often true that when a player in time trouble once misses a strong continuation, he will miss it again, should fortune so smile on him. 40...Qh1+ was again the move, as after 41.Kg3 Rg6+ 42.Kf2 (42.Kf3 Qxg2+ 43.Ke3 Qh3+ > 44...Qxc8) 42...Rxg2+, Black wins as before. Very easy to see with no clock ticking nearby. **41.Bxe7 Rxf4** 41...Rf7 loses to 42.d6 c2 43.Bxf8 Rxf8 44.d7. **42.d6 c2 43.Bxf8 Rxf8 44.d7** And that's that. All that remains for White to do is to endure a few checks, which he accomplishes easily. **44...Kh7 45.Rxf8 c1(Q) 46.d8(Q) Qh1+ 47.Kg3 Qe1+ 48.Kh2 Qe5+ 49.Kg1 Qe3+ 50.Rf2 Qc1+ 51.Kh2** Black Resigns.

Game 72: Jonsson=Horvath, Reykjavik Open 1982

1.e4 e6 2.d4 c5 3.d5 exd5 4.exd5 d6 5.Nc3 Nf6 6.Nf3 Be7 7.Be2 O-O 8.O-O Na6 9.Re1 Nc7 10.a4 Rb8 This game is a curious mixture of diverse positional ideas germane to the Barcza-Larsen. Here, for example, Black begins to prepare a queen-side advance, only to shift gears when White demonstrates similar intentions. **11.Bc4 b6 12.Rb1 Bg4** Left alone, Black would play ...a6 followed by ...b5, but White is threatening to break first on the queen-side with 13.b4, so Black simply tries to complete his development. **13.Bf4 Qd7 14.Nb5**

This maneuver is usually played in order to decrease pressure on the d5-pawn; here, it helps White give his light-squared bishop additional scope. **14...Nxb5 15.Bxb5 Qd8 16.Qd3 Ne8 17.Nd2** White prevents Black from exchanging bishop for knight. **17...Bg5** So Black opts for the exchange of the dark-squared bishops instead. **18.Qe3** If 18.Bg3, then 18..Bh4 and they dance 'til dawn (or drawn, by repetition). **18...Bxf4 19.Qxf4 Bd7** Exchange of the light-squared bishops normally favors White, but here, with reduced material (in particular, the missing dark-squared bishops) Black can defend successfully. **20.Ne4** There's no need to rush - White lets Black initiate the exchanging, which will result in a weak pawn on a7. **20...Bxb5 21.axb5 Rb7 22.c4 Re7 23.h3 Re5 24.Nd2** This allows Black to further relieve the pressure with additional exchanges, but Black did have the plan of ...Qe7 and ...f5, striking at the Re1. **24...Qf6 25.Qxf6 Nxf6** And not 25...Rxe1+ 26.Rxe1 Nxf6, because of 27.Re7! **26.Rxe5 dxe5** An instructive position. Black does have weak pawns at a7 and e5, but these can be defended; White can only attack a7 with his rook. White's queen-side pawns were devalued when Black played 20...Bxb5, so Black can await developments with confidence. **27.Ra1 Ra8 28.Kf1 Kf8 29.Ke2 Ke7 30.Kd3 h6 31.g4 Nd7 32.Re1** This permits Black to break on the queen-side, but it's the only active try. **32...a5 33.bxa6 Rxa6 34.f4 f6 35.Nf3 Kd6 36.fxe5+ Nxe5+! 37.Nxe5 fxe5 38.Rf1 b5 39.cxb5 Ra4 40.Rf7 Rb4 41.Rxg7 Rxb5 42.Rg6+ Kxd5 43.Rxh6 Rxb2 44.g5 Rg2 45.h4 Rg3+ 46.Kd2 c4 47.Rh8** Draw.

Game 73: D. Gurevich=Kavalek, US Ch. (Berkeley) 1984

1.d4 e6 2.e4 c5 3.d5 exd5 4.exd5 d6 5.Nf3 Nf6 6.Nc3 Be7 7.Be2 O-O 8.O-O Na6 9.h3 Nc7 10.a4 b6 11.Re1 Bb7 12.Bc4 Employing a different strategy than that seen in Balashov=Kasparov, Game 69, where White played Nf3-h2-g4. 12...a6 13.Nh4!? (And this is definitely a novel concept - White contemplates establishing the knight at f5, supported by g2-g4. 13...Re8 14.Nf5 Bf8 15.Rxe8 Qxe8 16.Bf4 Qd7 17.Qd3? Looks good, since it protects the Nf5 and frees up the Ra1, but 17.g4! was definitely better. 17...Bc8!

With this move, of a type notoriously hard to foresee, Black obtains the advantage. 18.g4 Gurevich was undoubtedly prepared to play this reinforcement, but 17...Bc8! had a twofold purpose: first, the obvious attack against the Nf5, but second, the self-blocking of the back-rank that makes a subsequent ...b5 possible. If 17...b5? immediately, White can exploit a tactical weakness along the back-rank: 18.axb5 axb5 19.Rxa8 and now Black's intended 19...bxc4 meets an even stronger zwischenzug, 20.Rxf8+! 18...b5! 19.Ba2 c4 20.Qd4 Bb7 21.Re1 White is losing a pawn, but Black must find the correct way to capture it. 21...Ncxd5 22.Nxd5

(See the diagram at the top of the next page)

22...Nxd5? And this isn't it! Black had to play 22...Bxd5!, with the possible continuation 23.Bg5 (23.g5? Qxf5) 23...Bb7 (Or 23...Re8!) 24.Bxf6 Qc6! 25.Kf1 Qg2+ 26.Ke2 gxf6. It's somewhat ironic that this winning procedure depended upon

yet another bishop retreat, 23...Bb7, to set up a powerful Q+B battery. **23.Bxd6!** An alert shot that wins back the pawn and leaves White with the better position. **23...Nf6** And not 23...Bxd6?? 24.Qxg7 mate. **24.Bxf8 Qxd4 25.Nxd4 Kxf8 26.c3 Ne4 27.Bb1 Nd2 28.Bc2 Nf3+ 29.Nxf3 Bxf3 30.Re5 Rb8 31.Kh2?!** White slips, allowing Black to reach an even end-game. The correct procedure would have been 31.axb5 axb5 (31...Rxb5 32.Rxb5 axb5 33.Kh2, when Black's pawns on b5 and c4 are weak.) 32.Rc5, intending Rc7. **31...bxa4!** Now White's b2-pawn is a weakness. **32.Bxa4 f6** But the pawn is not weak enough to permit 32...Rxb2?? 33.Re8 mate! **33.Re3 Bd5 34.Re2 g5 35.Kg3 Rd8 36.Rd2 Ke7 37.Bd1 Rd6 38.h4 h6 39.f4 Be6 40.Rxd6 Kxd6 41.hxg5 hxg5 42.Kf3** Draw. Because after 42...Bd5+ 43.Ke3 Kc5 44.Bf3 Be6! 45.f5 Bd5! 46.Be4 Bxe4 47.Kxe4 a5, neither side can break through.

Game 74: Hennigan+Cairns, CDS/Ceefax Junior Ch. 1987

1.e4 e6 2.d4 c5 3.d5 exd5 4.exd5 d6 5.Nc3 Nf6 6.Nf3 Be7 7.Be2 O-O 8.O-O Re8 9.Re1 a6 10.a4 Nbd7 Black adopts an old-fashioned, straightforward approach to his development, disdaining ...Na6/...b6/...Bb7 and instead preparing for immediate queen-side play. Should White bring a knight to c4, Black is prepared to challenge it with ...Nb6, and if White should attempt to prevent this with a4-a5, Black will simply play ...b5. **11.h3 Rb8 12.Nd2 Bf8 13.Nc4 Nb6 14.Ne3** White decides to over-protect the d5-pawn and block the e-file to avoid heavy piece exchanges. **14...g6** Black finds more suitable employment for his Bf8. **15.a5 Nbd7 16.g3?!** This is unnecessary. Since Black is prepared to play ...b5 and answer axb6 with ...Nxb6, White could eventually play Bf3 without worrying about ...Ne5. **16...b5 17.axb6 Nxb6 18.h4 h5 19.Ra3 Ra8 20.Nc4 Nxc4 21.Bxc4 Bg7 22.Rxe8+ Qxe8 23.Bf4 Ng4**

24.Qe2 24.Bxd6? Bd4! **24...Ne5** 24...Qxe2! 25.Nxe2 Be5 is better. **25.f3! Bb7?** The bishop has no future here and Black is forced to waste time defending it. **26.Rb3 Qd7 27.Ne4 Nxc4 28.Qxc4 Re8 29.c3 Re5?!** Both players were very short of time by this point. **30.Bxe5 dxe5 31.Qxc5 Bxd5 32.Rb8+ Kh7 33.Ng5+ Kh6 34.Qe3?** White missed an unstoppable mate after 34.Rh8+! Bxh8 35.Qf8+ Bg7 36.Qg8. **34...f5 35.Nf7++ Kh7 36.Ng5+ Kh6 37.Rd8 Qb7 38.Ne6+ f4 39.gxf4 Bxe6 40.f5+ Kh7 41.fxe6 Qe7 42.Rd7 Qxe6 43.Qa7 Qf6 44.Rf7 Qxf7 45.Qxf7** And after White survived a ten-move time scramble... Black Resigned.

Game 75: Chandler+Mikh. Tseitlin, Palma de Mallorca 1989

1.e4 e6 2.d4 c5 3.d5 exd5 4.exd5 d6 5.Nf3 Nf6 6.Nc3 Be7 7.Be2 O-O 8.O-O b6?! White's reply, in a position where move-order was long though unimportant, shows that a subsequent ...Na6 is inaccurate. **9.Re1 Na6?**

(See the diagram at the top of the next page)

This appears to be the real error. After 9...Bb7, White does not have recourse to his powerful next move. **10.Bb5!** White threatens the double attack 11.Qe2! **10...Nb8** A bitter pill to swallow, but 10...Nc7? fails to 11.Bc6 Rb8 12.Qe2. **11.Qe2 a6 12.Qxe7** And not 12.Ba4, because Black has the lateral defense

12...Ra7. **12...Qxe7 13.Rxe7 axb5 14.Bg5 Nbd7** 14...b4?
15.Bxf6 bxc3 16.Bxc3. 15.Nxb5 Nxd5 Black thinks he is regaining his pawn, since the rook surely has to move... **16.Nxd6!
f6** If 16...Nxe7, then 17.Bxe7 reclaims the exchange. **17.Nxc8
Nxe7 18.Nxe7+ Kf7 19.Nd5 fxg5 20.Nxg5+ Kg8 21.f3 Rae8**
(21...b5!?) **22.Rd1 Nf6!?** 22...Re2!? comes close to equality
after 23.Ne4 (>23...Rxc2 24.Ne3, with Rxd7 in the offing)
23...Ne5 24.Rc1 (With the threat of 25.Kf1) 24...Rxf3!
25.Ndc3 (25.gxf3 Nxf3+ 26.Kf1 Rxe4; 26.Kh1?? Rxh2 mate)
25...Rxc3 26.Nxc3 Rd2, but White has better in 23.Nc3!? Re7
24.Nge4. **23.Nxb6** 23.Nc3 Rd8! **23...Re2 24.Rc1 Rd8 25.Nc4
Rd4** 25...Nd5 26.Kf1 Nf4 27.Nh3. **26.Kf1** 26.b3 Nd5 27.Kf1
> 27...Nf4 28.Nh3. **26...Re7 27.b3 h6** 27...Nd5 28.Ne4.
28.Nh3 Nd5 29.Nf2 Nc3 30.a4! Rh4 31.h3 Na2 31...Ne2
32.Ra1 Ng3+ 33.Kg1 Rd4 34.Kh2 +-. **32.Ra1 Nb4 33.c3 Nc2
34.Rc1 Ne3+ 35.Nxc3 Rxe3 36.Ne4** White is now clearly
winning. **36...c4 37.b4 Rf4 38.Nc5 Rf5 39.a5 Rd5 40.Ne4
Red3 41.Ke2 Rb5 42.Ra1 Rd7 43.a6 Ra7 44.Nc5 Rb6 45.Ke3**
Black Resigns. If 45...Rd6, then 46.b5 Rd5 47.b6.

Index of Games

Players listed in CAPS had White.

Larsen+UNZICKER	Game 59
Levitina+ALEXANDRIA	Game 22
Levy-JAMIESON	Game 42
Ljiljak=STADLER	Game 16
LOTT=Gunderam	Game 9
MAKSIMOVIC-Hulak	Game 44
MARIOTTI+Cosulich	Game 25A
MASON+Anderssen	Game 2
MEYER-Hellenschmidt	Game 34
MEYSTRE+Klein	Game 43
MINCHIN+Trelawny	Game 1
MOISEEV+Bitman	Game 62
Moore-FIELDS	Game 45
MULLER-Bonsch	Game 20
MULLER-Stummer	Game 40
Murey=FEDOROWICZ	Game 35
NAVOJAN+Hachaturian	Game 66
NIKOLIC=Ristic	Game 23
NOBLESSE-Duthilleul	Game 8
O'KELLY-Larsen	Game 47
ORBAAN-Uhlmann	Game 53
Pahtz+BELKE	Game 29
PANNO+Barcza	Game 15
PORTISCH+Barcza	Game 60
PRIBYL=Gavrikov	Game 52
PROKOPP=Stummer	Game 46
Pronin-KARPOV	Game 37
Quinteros+TATAI	Game 67
Quinteros-VAGANIAN	Game 30
RAKIC+Todorcevic	Game 58
RANNIKU+Grinfeld	Game 19
REE+Wirthensohn	Game 26
Ristic=NIKOLIC	Game 23
ROSSETTO-Hubner	Game 63
RUBINSTEIN-Spielmann	Game 3
SANDOR+Barcza	Game 54
Sariego+ARMAS	Game 13
Savon-BALASHOV	Game 65
Savon-SMEJKAL	Game 25
Schmid=EVANS	Game 14
Schmid+VAN SCHELTINGA	Game 4
SCHULZ+Grossman	Game 12